J·HILLIER

UTAMARO

COLOUR PRINTS

AND PAINTINGS

PHAIDON

Phaidon Press Limited, Littlegate House, St Ebbe's Street, Oxford
Published in the United States of America by E. P. Dutton, New York

First published 1961
Second edition 1979
©1961 by Phaidon Press Limited

British Library Cataloguing in Publication Data

Hillier, Jack
    Utamaro, colour prints and paintings. – 2nd ed.
    1. Utamaro
    I. Title II. Utamaro
    769'.952   NE1325.K5
    ISBN 0 7148 1974 3
       0 7148 1975 1 Pbk

Library of Congress Catalog Card Number: 78–20503

Printed in Great Britain by Balding + Mansell, London and Wisbech

Acknowledgements

The author and publishers are much indebted to the following private collectors and museum authorities for permission to reproduce originals now or formerly in their possession: the Chester Beatty Library, Dublin (Figs. 56, 100); Mme Berès, Paris (Fig. 86); Mr Kiyoshi Shibui, Tokyo (Fig. 6); Mr F. Tikotin, Mont Pélerin, Switzerland (Figs. 2, 59); the Trustees of the British Museum, London (jacket illustration; Pls. I–V, VII, VIII, X, XII, XIV, XV; Figs. 5, 9, 14–19, 21–33, 35–41, 43, 44, 48–51, 55, 57, 58, 63–67, 69, 71, 72, 77–79, 87, 92, 95–99, 101–106, 108, 109); the Museum of Fine Arts, Boston, Mass. (Pl. IX; Figs. 47, 84, 85); Musée des Beaux-Arts, Brussels (Fig. 10); the Art Institute of Chicago (Figs. 20, 42, 90); the Wadsworth Atheneum, Hartford, Conn. (Fig. 11); the Honolulu Academy of Art, Hawaii (Figs. 54, 68, 75); the Victoria and Albert Museum, London (Pl. VI; Figs. 3, 4, 52, 62); the New York Public Library (Figs. 34, 73, 74); Bibliothèque Nationale, Paris (Figs. 13, 46, 53, 60, 88, 89, 91); the Smithsonian Institution, Freer Gallery of Art, Washington, D.C. (Fig. 83); Sotheby & Co. (Fig. 107); the Tikotin Museum of Japanese Art, Haifa, Israel (Figs. 45, 61, 76; tailpiece on p. 160; Pls. XI, XVI). Figs. 1, 7, 12, 81 and 82 are from originals once in the author's collection, and Figs. 93 and 94 from originals at present in his collection.

UTAMARO

CONTENTS

PREFACE

It is less true today than it was in 1961, when the first edition of this book appeared, to say that 'Utamaro's name does not come to mind as one of the great artists of the world'. If a Japanese artist's reputation is to be judged by the frequency of exhibitions of his work and by the invocation of his name in current art literature, only Hokusai can be said to rival Utamaro's standing, both in Japan and in the West. Yet so far as I can trace, no other monograph on Utamaro has appeared in a Western language since 1961, and though, in the light of the research and scholarship that have been brought to bear on the artist in recent years, my text may be faulted in detail, the general picture still seems valid, and the illustrations provide a truly representative selection from the immense *œuvre* of a consummate artist who is also a paradigm of what we understand by Ukiyo-e.

The Bibliography has been updated to include the very considerable quantity of books, articles and exhibition catalogues dealing specifically with Utamaro and his work which have been published since 1961.

J.H., December, 1978.

INTRODUCTION

IN LOOKING OVER the long list of Utamaro's achievements as a print-designer, a book-illustrator and a painter, we are inclined to view his work against the Japanese background only, to accord to it a high place among the productions of the Ukiyo-e masters, but no more. Utamaro's name does not automatically come to mind as one of the great artists of the world, as do those of say Rembrandt, Titian, Degas. Wide as our artistic sympathies have grown (the pioneers ever forcing the confines further afield, and the easy dissemination of reproductions in a host of books and journals consolidating the ground thus gained), they do not yet encompass the great artists of the East. The works of Eastern artists have not that currency among us, are not accessible, even in reproduction, to the great majority of art-lovers in the West, to whom the finest pictures of the great European masters have become 'household pictures'. A few of Hokusai's prints, like the *Hollow of the Deep-Sea Wave*, have attained to this universal acceptance, but very few others.

But there are other reasons for the relative ignorance concerning Eastern art. It has been persistently viewed as an esoteric art demanding for its proper appreciation a long and difficult initiation, as to some recondite cult—a view, it must be confessed, which some of the forbidding literature on the subject tends to confirm. Yet in no one other of the arts, certainly not in music or literature, with their formidable barriers of a tonal system and a language so remote from our own, does there exist such common ground for the interchange of ideas and ideals between East and West; and in these days of anarchy in art forms and concepts it would seem at least no more difficult for us to enjoy the paintings of Motonobu than those of Matisse, the colour-prints of Utamaro than those of Picasso: the Japanese artists are far less 'foreign' to our understanding than are the 'moderns' I have cited.

In regard to the colour-prints as distinct from the paintings of Japan there appears to be another misunderstanding, that being broadsheets produced for the masses, they are of little aesthetic consequence. The fallacy of this attitude is apparent if we consider the parallel case of Western prints which, at least until modern times, were, like the Japanese prints, a means of multiplying an artist's designs so that they could be sold cheaply to people who could not afford paintings. We do not now dismiss as of little importance the engravings of Dürer or the etchings of Rembrandt. The mediums by which a work of art may be produced have no ascending scale of importance: we derive more pleasure from the *Melancholia* than we do from any number of Dürer's oil paintings, and if the truth be told, is not the etching of *The Gold-weigher's Field* a finer landscape than the majority of Rembrandt's more ambitious landscapes in oils?

It is argued that the Japanese method was a reproductive one, that the colour-prints were not the work of painter-engravers, and it is, of course, admitted that as prints they lack the autographic quality of the true original etching or engraving. But wood-engraving has always largely been, in the West as well as the East, a reproductive process, and indeed, as a method of engraving in relief, it can never take the instantaneous impress of an artist's hand as the metal can: even Bewick's development of the 'white-line' wood-engraving merely converted the process into what might be called a negative one whereby a black print was achieved by white lines. In reproductive wood-engraving, the traditional, almost the sole, method of print-making in Japan, our admiration is not primarily for the engraving as such: although the colour-woodcut has a beauty of its own not translatable into any other medium, and a lover of Japanese colour-prints derives especial pleasure from the strength of the woodcut line and from the surfaces of flat colour, ultimately—even allowing, as we must, that the Japanese colour-prints from wood-blocks are technically the finest ever produced—the print's beauty comes from the designer's conception, the power of his brush-line, the originality of his composition. And in all these respects, Utamaro, at his best, is among the very elect.

As for those attributes of Japanese art which are its foreign accent in the universal language of art—

the emphasis on pattern and especially on a sort of 'irregular symmetry'; the conventionalizing of natural forms, including the human body; the arbitrary use of colour; the absence of chiaroscuro, of drawing 'in the round'; the rearrangement to the heart's desire of the disorder of nature—all these are characteristics that have now been absorbed into Western painting, and it was their very impact on European art in the nineteenth century that did much to turn our course from 'representation for its own sake', to re-orient us in directions that have led so far from the traditional paths followed since Giotto. Whistler's *Ten o'Clock* essay has passages that must have been inspired by recollection of Japanese prints; Bracquemond, Mary Cassatt, Toulouse-Lautrec and others came under the spell, and there exist paintings by Van Gogh that are literal transcriptions from colour-prints of the Ukiyo-e landscape-artist Hiroshige.

This absorption of certain characteristics of Japanese design into the European artists' technique, and the assumption that modern Western art is unlikely to find need for further borrowings from the same source, has given rise to an air of condescension on the part of some of our critics, who now tend to look on the Japanese colour-print as the product of a 'minor' art. By the same process, all the acknowledged great artists of the past, whose influence was once paramount but whose styles and methods are no longer current, might be relegated to the position of minor artists because painters 'since Cézanne' have no longer looked to them for inspiration.

But such paradoxes are frequently used to justify certain manifestations of modern art, and need not be taken too seriously. If it be agreed that neither the medium nor the size of a picture or print is of importance in assessing its aesthetic value, if qualities of draughtsmanship, composition and expressiveness are the ultimate bases of assessment, it is difficult to see why there should be this attempt to belittle the art of the masters of the Japanese colour-print. Great art is not the prerogative of any particular period, or race, or medium. The man who designed the lovely plates of the *Insect Book*, the *Shell Book* and other albums that claim the very highest place among the beautiful books of the world; who could invest an everyday happening like the *Women preparing stuff for dresses* with grandeur, and convey in a perfect composition like the *Fair sojourners at an inn* the soft intimacies of that twilight state between waking and dreaming; who could express in the *Awabi Fishers* the elemental nature of women close to earth; who devised compositions based upon single figures, or groups of two or three, of an originality that impresses us even now, though European artists, borrowing his ideas, have made commonplaces of his devices; who recorded his age and its pleasures with the same exquisite sensitivity that we admire in Watteau; this man Utamaro was a great artist by any standards.

CHAPTER ONE

THE SCHOOL OF TORIYAMA SEKIEN

It is difficult, and perhaps a little rash, for a European to attempt to write the life of a Japanese artist, especially one who died a century or more ago. Even in respect of those artists most venerated in Japan, the native records are scantier and less reliable than those at the disposal of an art-historian dealing with a minor artist in Europe, and concerning the Ukiyo-e artists there are few memorials of any biographical value. How unreliable the nearly contemporary accounts are can be judged by the fact that the date of Utamaro's birth is disputed; support can be found for at least four different birthplaces; and his death was for long confused with that of the publisher Tsutaya Jūsaburō, with whom he lived for some years.

Some will say that these details are irrelevant and unimportant: all we should be concerned with is the legacy of the artist, his works. Yet nobody can deny that a man's work takes on its full significance only in the light of the life we know him to have led, the impact of his environment on his art, the place of his work in relation to the social background of the period. So, however scanty the material, I have tried to piece together the known facts and the permissible surmises to give some substance to the shadowy figure we know as Utamaro.

It seems fairly well established that he was born in 1753, but there is no certainty concerning his birthplace, Kawagoe, Edo, Ōsaka and Kyōto all having been put forward plausibly at one time or another. Of his mother absolutely nothing is known: and the same must be said of his father, unless we accept the view that Toriyama Sekien was his father, as well as his master. About this, there has been endless controversy, one camp holding tenaciously to the view that Utamaro was the son, the other that he was simply the pupil of Sekien, and both producing telling evidence to support their arguments.

It may never be settled definitely one way or the other, but for our purpose at least it is granted that Sekien was indisputably Utamaro's father in art, and that, even if it were only by adoption, Utamaro became a member of his family. In Japan, such cases of adoption were not uncommon and the master did in fact seem to stand *in loco parentis* to the child-pupil.

Of Sekien, apart from his works, we know little. He was Edo-born, and was forty at the time of Utamaro's birth. He evidently came of a family rather above the social level of those normally enlisted in the Popular School, and as was fitting to such a one, had his initial training in the academic school of painting, the Kanō. In middle age, he began to show leanings towards the style of the Ukiyo-e or Popular School, and about 1770 established a school where he not only inculcated the Ukiyo-e method of painting but also a certain mode of seventeen-syllable poetry called *haikai*. Among his first pupils was Shikō, who, under the name of Chōki, produced a small number of exquisite colour-prints in the nineties. Sekiga, Sekihō and Sekijō are others of his pupils, whose work is comparatively rare and not particularly distinguished, but who indicate that Sekien's school was an establishment of some influence. His own work, apart from his paintings, mostly of his Kanō days and of no remarkable distinction, can be studied in certain rare books published from about 1770 until a few years before his death in 1788. Most of these are concerned with supernatural phenomena, the ghosts, monsters and hobgoblins (Fig. 1) with which Japanese legend and history teem, but a few have a more general subject-matter, the *kachō* (flowers and birds) being particularly successful. His style shows traces of his Kanō training to the last, and owing to the very nature of the subject-matter of his book designs, never wholly becomes Ukiyo-e in feeling. One book of his in particular, the *Sekien Gafu* of 1773, is much esteemed. In it, some of his finest designs are reproduced by a novel method of gradation colour-printing (Fig. 22).

From the old records we learn that 'he had a beautiful house and garden, where he was fond of entertaining friends at the ceremonial tea, at which he was considered an adept'. All told, he seems to have been a man of considerable attainments, accomplished in a number of the arts, and surrounded by all the refinements natural to a man of his station in the Edo of the eighteenth century.

1. Sekien: *The Goblin Spectre*. From *The Leisure-Treasure of 100 Goblin Utensils*, 1784.

It was in his household that Utamaro grew up, enjoying, we may be sure, as the ward of a man of Sekien's calibre, an education which took account of all the arts, and studying, in particular, the Kanō style of painting, which insisted above all on long practice in the use of the brush. Of this childhood we have one glimpse, an authentic one, vouched for by Sekien himself, of Utamaro in the garden of the Edo house, capturing insects and holding them closely in his hand to study them.

CHAPTER TWO

THE UKIYO-E SCHOOL AND
THE COLOUR WOODCUT

BEFORE GOING ON to the first known works from Utamaro's hand, it will be useful to explain references to 'schools' of painting, amplifying the terms *Tosa*, *Kanō* and *Ukiyo-e* which are bound to crop up from time to time.

In the Japan of Utamaro's day and for many centuries prior, divergent styles of painting with rigidly exclusive boundaries existed side by side. Painters were enrolled as young men in one or other of the great schools, and it was a matter of professional practice, and indeed of professional honour, to adhere strictly to the style, the method of painting, and with it often the particular range of subject, traditional to that school. It is difficult for us in Europe to realize quite how strong was the rule and authority of each of these particular schools, how strict the training necessary to acquire the mere technique before a painter could be accepted as an exponent of its tenets, or how unusual an apostasy from one school to another.

Until the seventeenth century, painting was an art largely performed and enjoyed by the restricted circle of the aristocracy, but it was widely appreciated within that circle—appreciation of painting was one of the accomplishments that every man of breeding was expected to possess, along with the ability to write an artistic hand, and to compose a neat verse extempore.

Up to that time, the two principal schools were the Kanō and Tosa, each identified with one of the opposing political factions, the first being associated with the Shōgun's circle, the other with the Emperor's. The Kanō school, with its roots in classical Chinese painting, specialized in idealized landscapes, *kachō* and scenes of myth or legend, often with some hint, veiled or explicit, of Buddhistic teaching; the Tosa, a more native product, repeated time and again scenes of court splendour, of civil war or romantic medieval adventure.

During the seventeenth and eighteenth centuries the work of both schools, for all the undeniable skill of the practitioners, was in a decline. The Kanō painters seemed content with repetitions, ever less

convincing, of the works of earlier masters, the Tosa employed the old conventional devices, such as the removal of the roof to lay bare the happenings within the Palace rooms, and the use of decorative gold bands across the sky, but, at this distance from the well-head of inspiration, with little of the narrative power and vigour of the ancients. Under the inspiration of painters too individualistic to submit to academic restraint, a number of separate groups emerged, each composed of men drawn together by similar aims and a common technique, of which schools the Ukiyo-e, Kōrin, Nanga, Shijō, Maruyama and Ganku are the most important. Of these we are concerned primarily with the first.

Simultaneously with the growth during the Tokugawa shōgunate of a new middle class or bourgeoisie composed of wealthy merchants, artisans and tradesmen, a new type of painting came into being, characterized not only by a style of brushwork and a conception of design differing from those prevailing at the time, but by a range of subjects hitherto only occasionally drawn upon, of a kind approximating to what we call *genre*. Although the name of Matahei Shōi was for a long time linked with the founding of the school in the seventeenth century, there is little evidence to support such a theory: the artists of the *Hikone Screen* and other works that mark the crystallization of the new style were anonymous artists for whose personalities and careers modern Japanese scholars make surmises with little reliable evidence. The style of the school, the outcome of a fusion of the Tosa and the Kanō, was adapted to the depiction in a novel way of the daily life of the capital, Edo, of the singing- and dancing-girls, of the courtesans, the wrestlers and the *Kabuki* theatre. The shallowness and the gaiety of its subject-matter earned the school its sobriquet *Ukiyo-ryū*, 'style of the floating world'.

The illustrated book became the principal vehicle by which this new and vital art was first brought into the homes of the common people, and from Moronobu onwards, wood-engraving, the

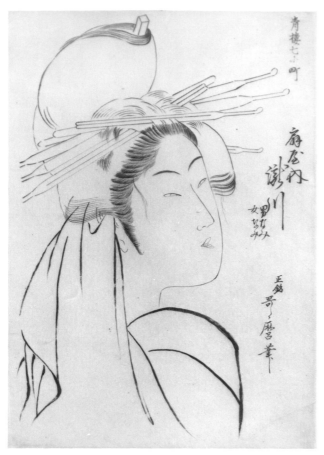

2. Original brush drawing for a print in the series
The Seven Komachi of the Green Houses. About 1796.

traditional Japanese method of reproduction, was
employed with increasing resource and accomplishment to reproduce the drawings of the Ukiyo-e
artists. At first, the engravings were in black outline
only. Then, when separately-issued sheets, broadsheets, began to appear, hand-tinting became the
custom, to further the likeness to original brush-
paintings. About 1741 the use of additional blocks
for printing colours was introduced, and after
various experiments with further blocks and over-
printing to secure additional tints, full polychrome
wood-block printing was achieved in 1764. It was
by then a perfect instrument for reproducing the
artists' designs and from Harunobu onwards until
the end of the century a succession of great artists
arose to take advantage of the superb medium
ready to hand, for whose novel and colourful products the Edo public was insatiate.

The process involved in producing these colour
woodcuts has been described a number of times,
but it is of such great importance to a consideration

of Utamaro's *œuvre*—by far the greater part of
which was in this medium—that I will briefly outline it again. It has usually been accepted that the
artist made his drawing on thin transparent paper
(Fig. 2), which was afterwards pasted face down on
to the surface of a prepared piece of cherry-wood or
similar close-grained wood and destroyed in the
process of cutting. However, certain outline drawings have survived that are unmistakably artists'
designs for the engraver, on paper of a thicker type
than that pasted on to the blocks, and it seems that
in some instances at least the artists' drawings were
copied in the engraver's workshop and the original
spared. Even so, very few such original drawings
have come down to us, and we can only conclude
that they were valued even less than the prints for
which they were made.

The engraver—never the artist himself—cut

3. A proof from a 'key-block'
inscribed with directions for colour in Utamaro's, or
possibly the publisher's, hand. Part of a triptych.
About 1804–6.

4. *Women making colour-prints*. Part of a triptych. About 1804–6.

around the artist's brushstrokes, afterwards cleaning the wood from between the lines, thus leaving them in high relief; another craftsman, the printer, now took over and first took impressions in black ink from the engraved blocks, thereby securing prints that were reproductions of the painter's original brush drawing (Figs. 3, 4). The artist now proceeded to indicate on one of these proofs where colour was to be printed, and the engraver then cut additional blocks, normally one for each colour. The master-printer, using watercolours mixed with a little rice paste, was then able to produce the full colour-print by imprinting each sheet successively on the six or eight or more blocks corresponding to the number of colours. Impressions were taken by hand, a twist of hempen cord called a *baren* being used to rub the back of the paper over each block. It was, in fact, entirely a hand process, and justifies Morrison's description of it as 'a process of water-colour by transfer'.

CHAPTER THREE

EARLY INFLUENCES AND FIRST WORKS

HARUNOBU ENJOYED an immense vogue from the time of the introduction of the full colour-print in 1764 until his death in 1770, and his daintily drawn and exquisitely coloured prints were on sale in every print-shop. No doubt many of them found their way into Sekien's home, with those of the other artists producing rival prints at the time, Koryūsai, Shigemasa, Shunshō and Bunchō especially, all to be eagerly studied by Utamaro and the other pupils of Sekien. True, Utamaro was only seventeen in 1770 and none of his works can be ascribed to so early a date, but he was not too young to take an intelligent interest in colour-prints, and though he was probably studying the Kanō style at the time, these attractive prints may already have turned his thoughts and inclinations away from the sterile academic repetitions to the more racy and fashionable Ukiyo-e. It may have been remembrance of what he owed to Harunobu in his youth that inspired him to design a print, some twenty-five years after Harunobu's death, in which he paid homage to the earlier master.

In this formative period, then, although Utamaro was under the tutelage of Sekien, who had a Kanō upbringing and never wholly outgrew it, he could hardly have failed to come into contact with the prints of the great Ukiyo-e masters practising at the time. What traces do we find of these influences in his early works?

Like most Ukiyo-e artists, Utamaro began his career by providing illustrations for various kinds of cheap popular literature—theatre publications, for

5. A page from the *kibyōshi* ('yellow-back') *Omi hakkei*. 1780.

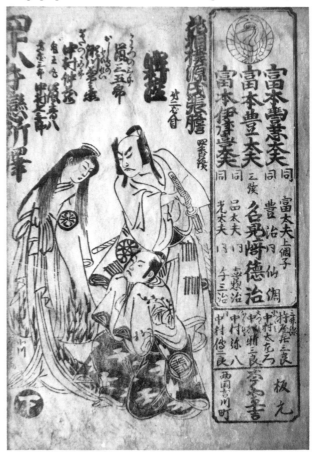

6. Title-page of the theatre-book *Koi-no-showake*, published in 1775, and thus Utamaro's first known dated work. Signed Kitagawa Toyoaki.

example, which gave details of subject and cast in the current productions, or novelettes and farces, known from their binding as *kibyōshi*, 'yellow-backs' (Fig. 5). The earliest known of these little books is dated 1775, and at this time, and for several succeeding years, the artist was using the signature Kitagawa Toyoaki. In Japan, a painter at the outset of his professional career assumed an 'art-name', which might be changed, and frequently was, by taking a name bestowed by a master, or as the outcome of a transfer of allegiance from one school to another, or as the result of what often appears to us to be mere caprice. Such changes provide one of the clues to the chronology of Japanese artists' work. Kitagawa was the family name of the publisher Tsutajū, with whom Utamaro took up residence about this time, and it seems that Utamaro adopted the name of his publisher and benefactor.

This theatre book of 1775 (*Koi-no-showake*) and similar books belonging to the years 1778 and 1779, have very little individuality (Fig. 6) and are only of interest because they are the earliest known of Utamaro's works, but they are nearest in style to that of the Katsukawa school of theatrical print designers. Few copies of these flimsy booklets exist; in fact, the preservation of any examples of such ephemeral literature is a matter for wonder. Cheaply produced on poor paper, the printing, in de Goncourt's phrase, '*un peu au diable*', they have none of the qualities of the fine prints on which Utamaro's reputation rests.

His contributions to these theatre books show that in his early days, Utamaro's pride did not preclude him, as it later did, from associating with the *Kabuki* or Popular Theatre, nor from depicting the actors in their favourite roles. Later, when he had become established, he considered it a point of professional pride to eschew the theatre, maintaining, so the tradition runs, that he did not wish his reputation to depend upon the fame of the actors portrayed, but solely upon his own artistic merits.

That sounds rather like the reflection of a man who has succeeded in one sphere and endeavours to account for his relative failure in another. The true reason for Utamaro severing his early connection with the stage may be found in other causes, not least of which, judging by extant examples of his work in this sphere, may have been an inability to compete with the established designers of theatrical prints. In the late seventies, the Torii

7. *The actor Iwai Kumesaburō in a feminine role.* About 1778–80.

school of artists, whose connection with the stage had been unbroken for nearly one hundred years, was represented by Kiyonaga, at this time a competent if not particularly impressive successor to Kiyomitsu: but it was Shunshō, of the rival Katsukawa school, then at the peak of his mastery, who was beyond question the outstanding artist of stage

8. *Hobgoblin with a lantern*. Probably about 1782–5.

other. Utamaro had not that precocity that marked a number of Japanese artists, Okumura Masanobu, for example. His art matured slowly and for a long time owed much to contemporaries.

Although Utamaro's work shows little of the Kanō style or of Sekien's own brand of Kanō-cum-Ukiyo-e—which might be accounted for by most of his earliest apprentice work having disappeared—there are traces of both. In landscape—usually, with Utamaro, only the background to his prints—he often shows the Kanō touch, and when, in an interior, he depicts a painted screen or *kakemono*, (see, for example, Pl. IV), it is invariably in the Kanō manner. But of all the landscapes having the Kanō impress, the finest occurs in the album of five prints entitled *Kyōgetsubō* ('*Moon-mad Monk*'), one print of which, of a rocky landscape with a waterfall and two small figures crossing a rickety wooden bridge, is in monochrome and a surprising essay in the Kanō style. And *Kyōgetsubō* was not published until 1789, long after Utamaro had reached his artistic majority. Moreover, as will be seen, the bold bravura of line characteristic of the Kanō academy gives a classical grandeur to courtesans masquerading as divinities in the series *Eight Charming Sages* (see Chapter XVI) and to many other subjects where the artist made game of the hallowed subjects of the aristocratic school.

Of Sekien's own range of subjects, his obsession with phantasmagoria, there is little trace in Utamaro's work. A few early prints of phantoms show that his master's mannerisms had been assimilated (Fig. 8) but Sekien had said practically all that could be said in this genre, and in any case it clearly did not attract Utamaro.

In 1777 appeared a book having for its subject the history of the Forty-Seven Rōnin, that parable, based on fact, of loyalty and self-sacrifice, whose immense popularity goes far to explain the fanaticism of the Japanese in war. The illustrations, signed Kitagawa Toyoaki, are undistinguished, and without the signature would not be recognized as Utamaro's work. The same can be said of the *kibyōshi* (see p. 33) which appeared in the next few years. The reproduction (Fig. 5) gives some notion of this particular class of work. As can be seen, the *hiragana* (phonetic) script was allowed to invade the drawing in a distracting way, and the engraving and printing are, by Japanese standards, third-rate.

prints. Only a few of the early theatrical *ichimai-e* (single-sheet prints) by Utamaro have survived. Perhaps the best preserved and the most interesting for the purpose of comparison with Shunshō is that in the British Museum (Pl. I). It is possible, fortunately, to date this print accurately. It represents the noted actor Yoshizawa Iroha in a play known to have been produced in the Nakamura Theatre in 1777, and the print was almost certainly issued at the same time or shortly after. It is quite a gracefully drawn little figure, but it falls into insignificance beside the splendidly dramatic prints of actors in character being produced by Shunshō at the time. Another print by Utamaro, signed Toyoaki and roughly of the same date as the British Museum print, is also reproduced (Fig. 7), and this is even feebler than the

I. *Yoshizawa Iroha in the play 'Sembon-Sakura', produced in 1777.*
Signed: Kitagawa Toyoaki.

II. *Boarding a Pleasure-barge. From Diversions of the Four Seasons. About* 1782–3.

CHAPTER FOUR

TSUTAYA JŪSABURŌ AND NEW INFLUENCES
1780 – 1785

THE EVENTS LEADING up to Utamaro's break with Sekien are never likely to be known, and there is no need to invent a quarrel as the reason for Utamaro deciding to leave his old master and to throw in his lot with Tsutajū. Whatever the reason, the move was a momentous one for the artist, then on the threshold of his career.

Tsutaya Jūsaburō, usually known as Tsutajū, began as a small bookseller with a shop near the main entrance to the Yoshiwara. He was a man of exceptional character, and his name is linked with some of the greatest artists, and the finest enterprises, of the Ukiyo-e school during the last part of the eighteenth century. He seems to have had not merely the gift of discovering genius, but the rarer one of prompting genius to yield its maximum. He was the sort of kindred spirit that must, in any case, have attracted Utamaro, and whether or not there was a family tie with Sekien, Utamaro was of an age to decide his own future. Besides, the arrangement to lodge with the publisher may have been a good business move, holding out the prospect of ample commissions, and contacts with the literary and artistic celebrities who formed the publisher's circle.

Utamaro's stay under Tsutajū's roof changed the whole direction of his life, and in the subtle way that rivalry and encouragement work—and he was subject to both during these years—his style veered this way and that before finding its own true tack on a course none had held before.

Several of Japan's greatest artists and writers became attached to Tsutajū's household, some, like the novelist Bakin and the author-artist Kitao Masanobu, seeking shelter under his roof after falling on evil days, and all apparently paying for their keep with the products of their art. Tsutajū was clearly much more than a clever publisher with an eye to business: generosity and warm-heartedness must also have been in his make-up. He himself was a writer of ability (his preface to the book of courtesans illustrated by Shunshō and Shigemasa is quoted below) and moreover he, more than any other publisher, was in the forefront of every progressive movement in art and letters. His house must have been a centre where a ferment of new ideas could distinctly be sensed, and that this charged atmosphere had a fructifying effect upon Utamaro cannot be doubted.

When Tsutajū moved to more commodious premises in 1783, encouraged by the response accorded to his publications by the Edo public (a public, as will be shown, seeking with growing feverishness the novel, the unusual, the bizarre), Utamaro followed him and continued to reside with him until the publisher's death in 1797. From 1783, the date of his removal, Tsutajū employed as his trade-mark a leaf of ivy (*tsuta*) beneath a triple peak—a mark that appears on many of Utamaro's most famous prints.

Before going on to describe Utamaro's work from 1780 to 1785, a word should be said, because of their impact on Utamaro, concerning the predominant forces in the Ukiyo-e school at the time.

When Koryūsai, representing what might be called the 'Harunobu period' of the colour-print, retired from active print-making about 1780, the leadership of the Ukiyo-e school seems to have been poised uncertainly between four artists: Shunshō, leader of the Katsukawa school of mainly theatrical print designers; Shigemasa, a fellow-pupil of Harunobu's under Shigenaga; Kitao Masanobu, his young but brilliant pupil; and Kiyonaga, the scion of the Torii family of artists, also hitherto mainly attached to the theatre. In 1780, Shunshō, at fifty-four, was already something of a veteran, and although the general standard of excellence he had maintained throughout his career was upheld until his death in 1792, he had no surprises in store, and, in fact, had never shown the temperament of a leader. Shigemasa, collaborator with Shunshō in the book of courtesans mentioned above, *Seirō bijin awase sugata kagami* ('*A Mirror of Rival Beauties*'), had the power and prestige to exercise great sway over his contemporaries. Although the younger partner in the book just mentioned, the references in it to the artists clearly show that of the two it was the younger that was considered of more consequence. Incidentally, the *Mirror of Rival Beauties* must have been one of the books well thumbed by Utamaro, and he must have been impressed by the beauty of its pages, elegantly composed and sweetly coloured designs of groups of courtesans engaged in the round of trivial occupations of the day. The preface to this book is by Tsutaya Jūsaburō and contains a statement that might well be taken as an expression of Ukiyo-e aims at this time. After mentioning an 'obscure Chinese saying to the effect that in painting the background is everything', Tsutajū contrasts with this the Japanese artists' preoccupation with 'the fashions of costume and hairdressing prevalent at each age, which pass as rapidly as the infant growing to manhood'. Many of the picture-books we admire so much were collections of fashion-plates, with the notable courtesans of the day as models.

A year or two after the publication of the *Mirror of Rival Beauties* Shigemasa designed some single sheets of *bijin*, 'beautiful women', which, though still linked with Koryūsai, have new harmonies of colour and composition, and as always with Shigemasa, supremely confident draughtsmanship. But for unknown reasons, Shigemasa seems to have preferred the illustrated book to the broadsheet, and his prints are comparatively few.

Kitao Masanobu, fellow-lodger with Utamaro at Tsutajū's, was originally a pupil of Shigemasa and his early work is very similar to his master's. But this 'marvellous boy' was more volatile than his master, whose steadiness and quiet resourcefulness remained with him until his death at a great age in 1819. Masanobu's rise was as rapid and spectacular as Utamaro's was slow and unremarkable. Apart from his tutelage under Shigemasa and his lodging with Tsutajū, little is known of his early life, though under the name of Santō Kyōden he later became one of Japan's most famous authors. Eight years younger than Utamaro, he was already illustrating *kibyōshi* at the age of seventeen, and in 1784, when he was twenty-one, Tsutajū published the extraordinary collection of seven diptychs of rival courtesans with specimens of their chirography—the *Mirror Comparing the Handwriting of New and Beautiful Courtesans of the Yoshiwara*—to be numbered among the half-dozen most beautiful Ukiyo-e colour-printed books. Straining the resources of the

9. Kiyonaga: *A boating party under Azuma Bridge.*
One sheet of a triptych. About 1785–6.

colour-print to the utmost, the designs owe their impressiveness to the great height and stateliness of the courtesans, an exaggeration Kiyonaga also employed with great effect, and which had its influence on all the Ukiyo-e artists of the nineties, Utamaro included.

Kiyonaga was a year older than Utamaro. Until the eighties, his work, though forceful and rarely uninteresting, had not had particularly outstanding qualities, nothing certainly to prepare one for the astonishing originality and masterly draughtsmanship that came soon after 1780. From then on he evolved a type of feminine beauty unsurpassed in the annals of Ukiyo-e—a sweetly expressive face, tall lissom figure, the grace and bearing of a goddess—and with this went a wonderful power of reposeful composition (Fig. 9). To some, he represents the culmination of the colour-print movement, and his finest prints, especially those in the two series *Brocade of the East in Fashion* and *Twelve Months in the South* are unquestionably among the supreme masterpieces of the colour-print.

These were the artists whose work was appearing during the period that saw the slow formation of Utamaro's style. Shunshō's influence, which can be seen in the early theatre-books and the separate *hoso-e* (narrow vertical prints) signed Toyoaki, was short-lived, and with but few rare exceptions, Utamaro afterwards eschewed the stage as a subject. Shigemasa, on the other hand, had a very strong influence, and close association with Masanobu, which I think can reasonably be taken for granted, resulted in Utamaro's work of the early eighties being strongly tinged with the style of these two artists.

Little apart from *kibyōshi* and other books in black and white has survived from the years 1775 to 1785, but a few rare single-sheet prints and still rarer diptychs belong evidently to the first half of the decade, and until the counter-influence of Kiyonaga begins to exert its effect, there is an unmistakable debt to Shigemasa and his pupil. There is a print reproduced in the Paris Catalogue[1] from a set entitled *Tsūsei Sanka no wata* ('*Popular Fashions in the "down-town" district of Ueno*'). It shows a girl negligently dressed in a black kimono flecked with white hachures leaning against a red wooden lattice, biting the end of her scarf as she places a long comb in her hair, and playing nonchalantly with a puppy clambering over her foot. Beside her kneels another girl in a pale violet dress with a young boy on her shoulder, whose attention she is trying to attract to a cicada in a cage, whilst he points excitedly to the puppy. The hair-style, the immaturity of the drawing and the composition generally stamp this print as belonging to 1780 or thereabouts, and the rather heavily jowled features of the girls, even the drawing of the wrists and hands, remind one instantly of Masanobu. An early *Niwaka* series, from which one print is reproduced (Fig. 11), must also be of this period.

But a diptych of this time is a memorable work, and deservedly praised by Binyon and Sexton as the finest of a number of extraordinary beauty and originality produced at this time. 'It is not quite the Utamaro with which we are familiar, but in essential qualities it owes nothing to preceding masters; it reveals already his genius for figure design, and considered simply in itself is an enchanting master-

piece.' This is not excessive praise: it is a print of April freshness, with the grace and refinement of Harunobu's idyllic world. It is fittingly entitled *Shiki asobi hana no iroka* ('*Diversions of the Four Seasons: the colour and fragrance of flowers*'). Whatever his triumphs afterwards, few of Utamaro's later prints have quite this morning freshness or this mood of innocent dalliance (Pl. II).

Another diptych of the same period is reproduced as Pl. 4 in the Vignier-Inada Catalogue. It shows a young *bon viveur* reclining on his side in a tea-house and blowing smoke from his pipe into the face of a girl who is serving him with tea. He is surrounded by girls ministering to his wants, and the central motif is a *tsuitate*, or standing screen, through whose transparent panels geisha girls with their *samisens* can be faintly seen.

In these two prints occur the earliest examples of the 'transparency motif' that was to reappear in many guises throughout the countless prints to come—a device that has a manifold effect, supplying a touch of realism that renders the most fanciful and exotic scenes believable, like the detail from everyday life that makes a dream convincing: pricking our curiosity to see beyond the veil; increasing the recession of the planes, one thing seen behind another serving to lead the eye into the picture; and causing unexpected changes of colour, like the face of the girl looking through an amber comb, or the courtesans retiring at night behind their green mosquito nets (Fig. 65), half bathed in the tender green shadow of the nets, half lit by the light of the lanterns.

Another print of some years later is of especial interest because it shows how intimate Utamaro was at this time with Kitao Masanobu, and gives an illustration of a rendezvous they both knew perhaps more than they should have done. This is a triptych entitled *Fête in a Tea-house* in which Kiyonaga's influence is already quite discernible. On the left, listening quite complacently to the proposals which a pretty girl is whispering close to his ear, is Kitao Masanobu (identified by the name on his sleeve), holding an inscribed fan in his hand. The inscription is a *kyōka*, a short comic verse: 'It's a good thing for a poet to be a bungler, for if his verses really had the power to shake heaven and earth, it would be most unfortunate'—an allusion to a medieval lyric affirming that the true poet has the power to make the sky and the earth

---

[1] Then in the Vever Collection, now in the Ueno Museum.

10. Left-hand sheet of a triptych known as *Fête in a Tea-house*, with a representation of
Kitao Masanobu, kneeling and holding a fan. 1786–8.

tremble. Nearby a little girl titters at the couple
from behind a screen, and all around there is the
bustle and the slightly tipsy gaiety which this evening of licence, with its free-flowing *sake*, has en-
gendered (Fig. 10).

From what Kitao Masanobu drew—his *Auto-
graphs of the Courtesans* and those two delightful
books published in 1786 and the following year of

pictures of the comic poets, *A Sackful of Humorous
Poems* and *A Bookcase of Humorous Poems*—and
from his poetry and novels written under the name
of Kyōden, one is bound to conclude that Masanobu
in his twenties must have been a companion of
great charm, witty, laughter-loving and intellectual
beyond his years. Of his appeal to Utamaro there
can be little doubt: and that they should have been

11. *Geisha preparing for a carnival.* About 1782.

boon companions reflects not only Utamaro's pre-dilections but also something in his own make-up that appealed to Masanobu. Perhaps it was a common love of the *sake* cup and the society of pretty girls: but it may also have been common sympathies and enthusiasms, and, at the time, similar aims in art.

But unaccountably, Masanobu practically forsook painting and print-designing for literature just when he seemed about to assume the leadership of the Ukiyo-e school, and at an age when others were usually no more than at the outset of their careers. After the age of twenty-seven he turned only occasionally from his writing to provide illustrations for books, and never with quite the flair he had shown as a youth.

By the mid-1780s on the other hand, Kiyonaga was producing a series of masterpieces that seems

12. Fan: *Night Rain*, from a series *The Eight Views Represented by Popular Fashions of Women*. About 1786–8.

to have enthralled the Edo public and to have won over to his style every artist of note. There are prints by Utamaro that can be ascribed to this period with so pronounced a Kiyonaga look that they are, for all their beauty, uncharacteristic, certainly not the real, unmistakable Utamaro who was soon to emerge.

Perhaps Utamaro is nearest to the Kiyonaga ideal in two prints of a party of women at the foot of the steep rise of the Ryōgoku Bridge across the Sumida river (Fig. 13). The girls are taller, more willowy than those appearing in Utamaro's books at this time and though not on the grand scale of Kiyonaga's Junoesque figures, undoubtedly owe much to his inspiration.

Another beautiful print by Utamaro of this period with a Kiyonaga flavour is a triptych of a

summer evening on the Sumida. In the foreground a pleasure-boat is about to bump the jetty. Sprawled on the top of the timber cabin is a raffish young spark with a *sake* cup in his hand. Another of his kidney below tips the dregs of his *sake* overboard. Around them, charmingly disposed to show to the best advantage their lovely garments, are the numerous feminine companions of these two sprigs of Edo youth. Beyond their tall figures can be seen the crowded traffic of the river and the whole Sumida river-front, dwellings, wharves, landing stages, boat-houses among a line of dark trees, and just at the left, the first piles of the Ryōgoku Bridge.

Into these prints, Utamaro has brought that 'plein air' atmosphere that had been one of Kiyonaga's greatest contributions to the colour-print, and the figures are bathed in the softly sunlit

13. *An outing on the banks of the Sumida*. About 1788.

14. *The Three Chinese Heroes pledging their Friendship.* About 1788–90.

air of the Edo summer. But whatever the debt to Kiyonaga, this triptych has qualities entirely its own in the composition, in the masterly disposition of the figures to give continuity to the design, and in a sort of dynamism, a latent liveliness, that is quite distinct from Kiyonaga's more static, sculpturesque groupings.

It was Kiyonaga, however, who remained the publishers' star attraction, and Utamaro stayed relatively in the background. Perhaps it was this partial eclipse that persuaded him to turn his attention to the picture-books, the *Insect Book*, the *Shell Book* and the *Bird Book* and the albums to be described shortly; and perhaps, too, the small number of prints having Chinese subjects (Fig. 14) were novelties intended to attract attention. Utamaro was, it is true, now a recognized master. In

1784 a spate of *kibyōshi* was published—at least six are known—and Hayashi (one of the earliest investigators of Utamaro's work and the inspiration behind de Goncourt's book of 1891) thought he saw evidence that many of the drawings had been prepared *before* 1784, and that Utamaro's success caused them all to be published at this time. In the following year, he is known to have had at least three pupils, Mitsumaro, Yukimaro and a woman artist Chiyo-jō, who all published *kibyōshi* with that date. In 1787, Sekien's references, too, are plainly to an artist accepted as outstanding in his profession. None the less, Utamaro may have felt a need to assert himself, to make a mark in a new direction beyond the reach of rivalry, aspirations resulting in the lovely *Insect Book* and the succession of albums soon to be described.

CHAPTER FIVE

EDO IN THE 1780s

IT MUST NOT be considered surprising that we have little biographical data for these years. Although Utamaro had evidently, in 1785, arrived at a position of some consequence in the Ukiyo-e school of painters, he was still, to the world at large, little different from an artisan, a carpenter say, of whom no written memorials were likely to be left. But of the Edo of his day, the kind of life he can be expected to have led, the social round he moved in, of all this the picture-books and prints give us a wonderfully detailed account. Edo in the eighteenth century may have lacked diarists like Pepys or Parson Woodforde, but it is safe to say, I think, that no town and its people, even in Europe, were so constantly depicted.

'Depicted' is perhaps an equivocal word to use as it begs one of the questions that confronts us in any consideration of Utamaro's art, as to how far he recorded the Edo of his time, and how far he pictured something based on Edo and its inhabitants, but really a dream world of his own imagination. We can hardly think of an Ukiyo-e artist, as we might of a European genre painter of the same period, as the camera-eye whereby we are able to view a world otherwise lost to us. Utamaro's art is the very antithesis of the literal photograph: it is an art that wills rather than accepts, that selects, composes and translates, making the everyday memorable, the prosaic poetic. Indeed, it might be argued that so far from attempting a literal rendering of the contemporary scene, he was more concerned to distract people from the realities of their surroundings.

A glance at the reproductions of Utamaro's prints in this book gives us an impression of a land of colour, of grace and of pleasure-going, of exquisite women attired in sumptuous garments displayed with all the elaborate coquetry of the

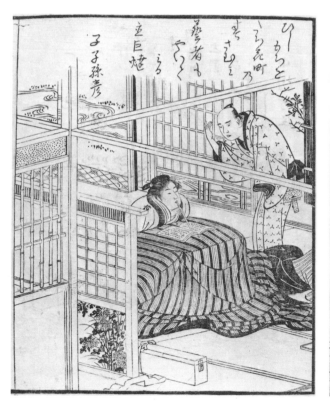

15. *Interior of an Edo house*, from the picture-book *The Edo Sparrows (or 'chattering guide')*. 1786.

16. *Street scene*, from the picture-book *The Edo Sparrows*. 1786.

mannequin's art, and where, if the mere male appeared, he was either as beautifully garbed as the women and as much dress-conscious as they, or else a menial in a loin-cloth, whose weather-beaten and hairy limbs acted as a foil to the fashionable pallor of the women and their effeminate consorts; of an amorous and wine-bibbing people forever bent on pleasure, with an inordinate love of festivals and gay shows of every kind, Edo itself being a carnival capital more often than not *en fête*.

These are the impressions, I think, that Utamaro's prints give us of the Japan of the eighteenth century. But what, in sober historical fact, was the Edo of that time like, and what sort of people were they in the capital, and how did they really live?

We find that Edo was the capital of what we would now call a police-state, with many of the evils we have come to associate with totalitarianism —repressions, secret police, rigid censorship, and banishments; and with the additional drawback that the dictator, the Shōgun, became so by right of primogeniture. Iyeharu and Iyenari, who held this office during Utamaro's working career, were dissolute creatures whose policies, or lack of them, brought the country to ruin. Position and office fell

to favourites who had bought their way by bribery into the Shōgun's affection; and with few exceptions, such place-seekers were unfit to govern. The bribery and corruption strained the finances of the Daimyōs, who levied harsh taxes on the people to recoup their fortunes, frequent peasant revolts proving how cruelly the Daimyōs' subjects were squeezed.

Then, just at a time when maladministration and corrupt government had already brought the country to the edge of disaster, there was a series of natural calamities. In the summer of 1783, for instance, when Kiyonaga was at the height of his powers, and his lovely diptychs depicting untroubled women and their consorts amusing themselves in the Edo pleasure-grounds were all the rage, and when Utamaro was designing such idyllic prints as the *Boarding a Pleasure Barge* (Pl. II) —could anything, we ask ourselves, be amiss in such a world?—in this summer of 1783 Asamayama erupted, earthquakes followed, and all that part of the country was engulfed in a catastrophe of the first magnitude, vast areas of agricultural land being ruined and widespread famine resulting.

Yet Iyeharu's harem at the time has been

17. *Gambling in the rice-fields*, from the picture-book *Tatoe-no-bushi*. 1789.

likened to the Parc aux Cerfs of Louis XV. Murdoch, who is the reverse of sensational, wrote: 'In the penultimate decade of the Eighteenth Century, Edo banquets were characterised by even a deeper measure of sumptuous dissipation than any of the "little suppers" in contemporary Versailles or Paris, and while no less extravagant, they descended to lower depths of licence and worse forms of depravity. Gambling was also common and involved as high stakes in Yedo as in Paris, and the austere characteristics of the samurai in the days of Kiyomasa and Yoshimune seemed to be replaced by those of profligate and self-indulgent roués, eager to acquire money, which it was formerly the proud samurai's boast to despise, by any means, for the gratification of their vices.'[1]

The years 1780 to 1792 are noted in the annals of Japan as a period of starvation and misery. The year 1787 in particular was marked by one of the worst famines in the history of Japan, and owing to the cornering of the rice by unscrupulous merchants, the price of what food there was was quite beyond the means of a large proportion of Edo's vast population of well over a million souls. The plight of the

[1] *A History of Japan*, Vol. III. *The Tokugawa Epoch, 1652–1868.*

poorer people can well be imagined. Mob-violence became frequent, gangs of desperate *komusō* (*samurai* outlaws) and the bolder spirits of the common people broke into the merchants' shops and go-downs and looted what they were unable to acquire honestly to keep them and their families from starvation.

One could retail from the history books many harrowing stories of dissoluteness in high places and distress in low, of extremes of wealth and want. Enough has been said to prove that the impression that Utamaro's prints give of a world of graceful dalliance and uninterrupted pleasure, is an illusion, and his pictures can no more be relied upon for a realistic representation of the contemporary scene in Edo than Dufy's can be accepted as a faithful record of Paris and its people today. In fact, a case could be made for them as 'escapist' pictures, popular in proportion to their distance from the unpleasant facts of existence.

During the troublous years I have mentioned, Utamaro made the designs for a number of picture-books that have Edo and its environs as their subject-matter, and which seem to have been produced as souvenirs of the capital. Almost every Ukiyo-e artist of note has left at least one or two

18. *The fish thieves*, from the picture-book *Tatoe-no-bushi*. 1789.

of these little books, usually in black and white, though colour-printing was occasionally employed. With their aid, we walk the streets of Edo, mingle with the colourful noisy crowds, watch the frequent passing processions, perhaps a great Daimyō and his retinue, or the beauties of the Yoshiwara 'on parade'; take our place in one or other of the tea-houses and listen to the music of *samisen* and flute. Owing to the recurrence of earthquakes, Edo consisted of long lines of low erections, mainly of timber. It was a place of beautiful gardens where trees of a multitude of species, especially those with showy blossom, cherry, plum and peach above all, were planted, invariably with a guardian pine—no view of the town but at least a few clumps of trees are visible, distant vistas invariably being closed with a feathery horizon of dark conifers, the houses dotted among them. The light, open timber work, the unfailing colour, give us the impression of a 'pleasure garden' with its gay pavilions, impermanent and fancifully designed tea-houses, and temple gates that could never have been associated with any exacting or severe religion; an impression completed by the jostling crowds of festively clad women, men and children who throng the avenues

and the 'houses of refreshment'. The river is never far distant. Masts and rigging appear beyond the roof-tops in nearly all the panoramas and street-scenes, and the artists took an especial delight in depicting the water-front and the busy traffic of barges and pleasure boats plying up and down. The Ryōgoku and the Nihon-bashi, wooden bridges on great piles, recall the lines of old Battersea Bridge as Whistler depicted it, with memories probably of the old Edo bridges in mind.

In 1786 Utamaro drew the pictures for a little book of this kind called *Edo Suzume* (Figs. 15-16), a title which seems to carry a number of implications, for it can be translated 'Edo Sparrows', and as such suggests 'bird's-eye' views, or else '*Chattering Guides*', which more or less conveys the purpose of the book. In the three little volumes forming this work there are views which seem to have been taken from the fire look-out posts on the roof-tops, the figures in the streets reduced to ant-like proportions. There are pictures of the beach in Edo Bay; of boating parties on the Sumida river; of girls disporting themselves in the Edo hills armed with fans with which they prettily, but ineffectually, strike at fireflies; and of travelling vendors of food

19. *A gathering of friends at Miho-no-matsubara*. A print issued to commemorate the entry of Shurakusai Takimarō (seen in the *kago* to the left) into the circle of Yoshiwara poets in 1787.

20. *Hinazuru and two kamuro girls looking at a painting representing Fukurokuju*. From the book *Collected Poems of Kamakura-no-Chikabitō*. 1787.

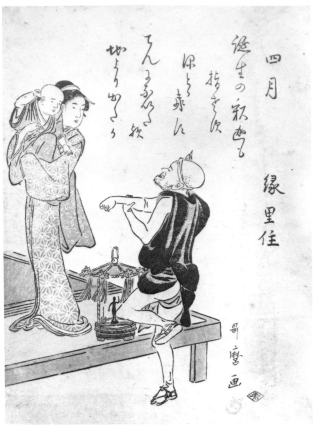

四月

縁里住

誕生の新茶で
指をちよ次
ほ女ら気に
ようなるか
かちら切り

哥麿画

21. *A mendicant priest asking for alms
on the 'Birthday of the Buddha'*. About 1785–6.

who have set up their stalls at the end of the
Ryōgoku Bridge, the customers standing and eating
rice from bowls. One looks in vain for the misery
and starvation that the history books assure us
afflicted the people at this time.

Another rather similar publication of 1789 is
entitled *Ehon Tatoe-bushi*, in which scenes from everyday life (Fig. 17) alternate with illustrations from
ancient history and legend. Although the effects of
famine must still have been all too evident in Edo,
Utamaro contrives to ignore it, or to make light of
it. A number of comedies in the streets are depicted
with gusto. In one snow scene, a fishmonger leaves
his basket to chase a dog that has run off with a fish
in its mouth, one of his unscrupulous customers taking the opportunity to extract another fish from the
basket on the end of a stick (Fig. 18). And that is the
nearest that Utamaro comes to commenting on the
conditions of the time. One can imagine how Goya
might have depicted this Edo and its inhabitants,
with what ferocity we would have been made aware
of the wasted forms, the hollow eyes and the
protruding ribs.

Still, these little books are admittedly 'guides' and
if they were intended as souvenirs of a visit to the
capital we would hardly expect them to give other
than a series of flattering views. It is more in the
many series of separate prints and in the albums and
picture books produced for internal consumption
rather than 'export' that the escapist attitude I
have mentioned seems most pronounced, this crea-
tion of a fictive world peopled largely by women,
especially women of the pleasure quarter. To understand the demand for this type of print and book
we have to know something of the people for whom
they were produced. What can be said of the
people of this town, among whom Utamaro strolled
with Masanobu, bandying pleasantries with the
beauties as they passed, noting with the artist's eye
for detail the lilt of their walk, the gesture as the
umbrella is opened against the sudden shower, the
ruffling of the silks as the wind sharpens?

Judging by the prints, the chief characteristics
were playfulness and pleasure-seeking, a love of
colour and of fine dresses, a passion for shows,
pageants, festivals and fêtes, a veneration of the
moon, of snow, of flowers, a nature-worship that led
them in parties on pilgrimages to see the flowering
cherry-trees or to watch the rising of the full moon:
child-like tendencies, some might hastily conclude,
but bespeaking perhaps an innate sense of the
beauty around and something unspoilt in natures
that seemed to look beyond the mere 'getting and
spending' and found the true business of life in
pleasure. This Edo has been dubbed the 'Paris of
the East', and in respect of its culture, its restless
seeking after new refinements in its amusements,
there is some justification for the comparison.

It seems generally agreed now that a far wider
section of the populace than was for a long time
admitted was patron of the Ukiyo-e artists. It was
not only the *heimin*, the common or working class
people, who purchased the prints and the albums.
For one thing, the rigid barriers which had existed
until the eighteenth century between the aristocrat
and the commoner began to break down. The
samurai, caught up in the vicious system whereby
place went to the highest bidder, and needing at all
costs to keep up 'appearances', were often hopelessly in debt, and the practice of marrying into
wealthy merchants' families or adopting sons of
those families into their own became common
expedients to avoid bankruptcy or brigandage, the

alternatives. Besides, whatever may have been the martial character of the samurai earlier, by now it was no longer proof against the blandishments of the pleasure centres of the town, or against the allure of the colour-prints and books.

The Ukiyo-e artist catered, in fact, for many tastes. For the least cultivated minds, there were the *kibyōshi*, the 'yellow-backs' which were little more than strip cartoons in booklet form. For tradesmen, artisan and man-in-the-street with an eye for colour, there were the stock prints of courtesans, which we need not hesitate to liken to the 'pin-ups' in vogue here today, and the prints of the actors in the latest thrillers being performed on the *Kabuki* stage. For those with a more advanced taste in literature there were the *yomi-hon* or reading books, novels like those of Santō Kyōden or Jippensha Ikku, in which text and illustration were on equal terms. For the sophisticated wits and poets, for the wealthy merchants and the samurai, there were the finely produced poetry albums (Chapters IX, X) and the more lavishly printed broadsheets and *ehon* (picture-books); and for all types, and for all pockets, there were the books of *shunga* or erotic pictures.

'Strip-cartoons' and 'pin-up girls' are rather belittling terms, but the comparison they suggest does bring out the resemblance of the class that favoured the diverting products of the Ukiyo-e artists to the class that nowadays devours the products of the sensational press, aimed at those with a low mental equipment who turn from their humdrum occupations to the 'comic strips', to the more lurid crime reports and to photographs of film-stars and sporting celebrities.

A large proportion of the colour-prints, however, seems to have been directed to a remarkably intelligent and quick-witted audience. As Mr Volker has written: 'It was a remarkable public, that of Tokugawa Edo. Even the very humble, through professional story-tellers and through the theatre, were quite familiar with the legends of their country and the history of ancient days as well as with religious personages of China and even of India, with classic poetry and with country songs and dances as well as with the folklore specific to various places all over the land.'[1]

But there was a noticeable streak of irreverence, if not of cynicism, in Utamaro's public, something of that odd manifestation we call *fin-de-siècle*, a sort of weariness with rationality, an intolerance for things as they are, a craving for the spice of novelty, for the scandal of impropriety. Nothing was sacred to Utamaro, myth, legend, history or religion. The heroes of the Chūshingura, deified among the people as the types of loyalty and courage, were 'guyed' in several sets of prints in which their deeds of derring-do are brought down to the level of brawls in the brothels; the Eight Immortals of Chinese legend are travestied by Yoshiwara beauties; even the great Taikō himself could not escape Utamaro's ribaldry, and for defying the censorship by naming Hideyoshi and other sacrosanct worthies on prints that showed them in anything but an heroic light, Utamaro actually earned a period of imprisonment, as will be described later. There is little doubt that pictorial *double-entendres* were as much admired in prints as puns were in poetry; burlesque and parody, oblique references rather than direct statements, any departure from the simple unvarnished truth, was welcomed.

[1] Ukiyo-e Quartet.

CHAPTER SIX

THE 'INSECT BOOK'
1788

IN THE YEAR 1788 appeared the first of Utamaro's works that had the stamp of indisputable originality, owing little to the acknowledged masters of Ukiyo-e—the book of colour-prints called *Ehon Mushi Erabi* (*A Picture Book of Selected Insects*), two volumes containing between them fifteen double-page prints, each having for its subject a flowering plant or a fruit, and one or more insects or reptiles (Figs. 23–26; Pl. III).

The book opens with a short preface by one Yadoya Meshimori, who is also responsible for the selection of humorous poems one of which appears on each print. A word should be said about these verses, *kyōka*, as they were the origin of many lovely books illustrated by Utamaro and other Ukiyo-e artists.

The *Insect Book* was furnished with verses by a club of comic poets, such clubs being a common feature of Utamaro's day. Anyone with any pretensions to wit had to be able to indite *kyōka*, literally 'mad verses', to order. This taste for 'occasional verse' illustrates another side of the character of those forming Utamaro's circle—a flair for dabbling in the arts, a sort of universal dilettantism which accounts for the enormous legacy of verses and albums of sketches which, one feels certain, were the work of gifted amateurs. People were not content to be mere onlookers of the arts but aspired to be executants, banding themselves into clubs, often under some master of the art, to practise *kyōka*- or *haikai*-writing, or *koto*- or *samisen*-playing, or the arts of calligraphy or flower-arrangement.

At the end of the *Insect Book*, the publisher advertised the fact that it would be followed by books on birds, animals and fish, and stated that the subjects would be announced in advance, so that

22. *Cicada, egg-fruit and beanflower*, from Sekien's picture-book *Sekien Gafu*. 1773.

III. *Locust on bamboo fence with flowering plants*, from the *Insect Book*. 1788.

IV. *A monkey-trainer putting his animal through his tricks in a nobleman's house. From the album* Young God Ebisu. *1789*

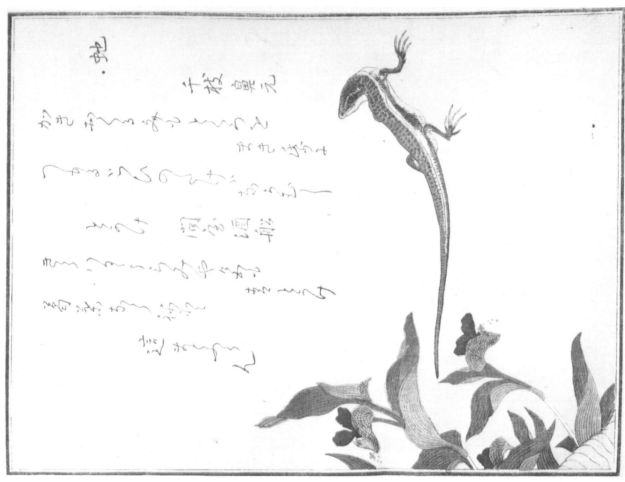

蛇

23. *Snake, lizard and Notarugusa bush.* From the *Insect Book.* 1788.

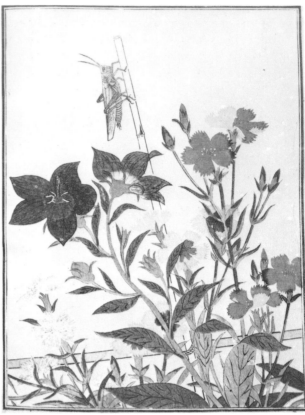

24. Red dragon-fly and locust on bamboo fence. From the Insect Book. 1788.

those versifiers who wished to submit their work might compose their *kyōka* according to the subject. *Momo-chidori*, Utamaro's *Bird Book*, appears to have been supplied in this way.

The *kyōka* are seldom in what we would call good taste, and the writers invariably managed to bring the most unpromising subjects round to matters hardly fit accompaniment for innocent pictures of birds or shells. We foreigners are in rather better case than the Japanese themselves for enjoying the pictures in these books where the *kyōka*, in flowing *hiragana* script, is no more to us than part of the decoration of each page, most of us being spared the meaning of the graceful calligraphy. A suggestive verse, plain for all to read, would be fatal to the detachment in which we appraise the purely aesthetic merits of the designs. For some Japanese, such highly seasoned garnishing seems to have heightened their enjoyment of the prints.

The popularity of the *kyōka* at this time as a means of expression is significant. Kenji Toda, the compiler of the Ryerson Catalogue[1], has an interesting passage on the subject. 'Why did this kind of

[1]See Bibliography, p.159.

poetry,' he asks, 'so flourish at this particular period? In the first place it was a reaction to the poetry of the classical school, which, with its strict rules and elaborate technicalities, ceased to be a real expression of life. Social conditions then permitted all classes of people the chance to seek certain cultural enjoyments, but the classical field was too exclusive and unattractive. It was natural for people to take to this easier and more interesting accomplishment. The general trend of that sophisticated age was also favourable to the enjoyment of such merry-making in poetry. A majority of the people avoided serious thoughts, and light refined humour was what most appealed to them. The meetings of *kyōka* poets served as a kind of social club for those care-free people to while away their leisure hours with joking in poems.'

At the end of the prints is Toriyama Sekien's postscript, already referred to and here given in full:

'To reproduce the images of living things in the mind and to draw them with the brush is the true art of painting. In the work we now publish, my pupil Utamaro reproduces the very life of the world of insects: it is indeed true "painting from the heart". And when I remember times past, I recall that since his childhood little Uta observed the minutest detail of things. Thus, in the autumn, when he was in the garden, he set out to capture insects, and be it cricket or grasshopper, if he made a prize, he would keep the little creature in his hand, and amuse himself by studying it. And how many times I have scolded him, fearing he might get into the way of killing these living things.

'Now he has acquired his great skill in painting, he has made these studies of insects the glory of his profession. Yes, he manages to make the lustre of the firefly shine out in a manner to stagger ancient painting; he borrows the tiny weapons of the grasshopper to make war for him and puts to good use the earthworm's powers to undermine the old edifice. He thus seeks to penetrate the mystery of nature with the blind groping of the larva, lighting his way with the firefly, and getting himself out of the tangle at last by grasping the end of a filament of a spider's web.

'He has faith in the publication of the *kyōka* of the Masters; whilst, as to the merit of the engraver, it is the work of the knife of Fuki Kazumune.

'The winter of the Ram year of Temmei (i.e. 1787).

Toriyama Sekien.'

One interesting deduction, in considering Utamaro's character and certain aspects of his work, can be drawn from the rather high-flown hyperbole of the peroration. This was nothing less than a gauntlet thrown down to the 'established' schools of painting, particularly the Kanō, whose adherents had for centuries excelled in the painting of flowers and birds, but whose style, by Utamaro's day, had become flat and stale, and in need of some fresh inspiration. Sekien, himself brought up in this very school, was quick, with the apostate's willingness to do injury to his old faith, to seize an opportunity to elevate the humble Ukiyo-e school at the expense of those favoured by official recognition, and no doubt hoped that Utamaro's prints would 'stagger ancient painting' and 'undermine the old edifice'.

And behind Sekien's words we can discern Utamaro's pride: a pride in his prowess that had decided him to this contest, the pride that made it impossible for him to admit to the superiority of the Kanō school simply because of its ancient origin and aristocratic protagonists.

In making his challenge, Utamaro had chosen his field well. I think it can be truthfully said that no nation in the world has given more open worship to nature, to the beauties of nature—the moon, snow,

25. *Cricket on polygonum and fireflies on and above yoshi reed.* From the *Insect Book*. 1788.

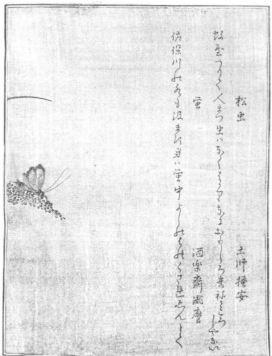

flowers, birds, the mountains, waterfalls—than the Japanese. It runs through their art and literature like a religion and indeed, it almost amounted to that in their daily lives. The veneration in which they held certain birds and animals, the lore of flower-arrangement, the pilgrimages to greet the new moon or to see the cherry-trees in flower in spring and the red leaves of the maple in autumn, the love amounting to deification almost of the peerless mountain, Fuji; all these observances were made with a religious intensity, each had a ritual, its canons of performance to which adherence was strictly given.

That absorption with landscape characteristic of Japanese painters from the earliest times can be ascribed to this deep-seated reverence for the beauty around them; a cultivation of such a reverence was, indeed, an article in the faith of the Zen sect of Buddhism, itself a potent influence in the arts. And so, too, we find the paintings of 'flowers and birds', the genre called *kachō-e*, imbued with the mysticism of a nature-loving cult, for a parallel to which, in this country, we have to go to another art, that of poetry.

'To me the meanest flower that blows can give
Thoughts that do often lie too deep for tears.'

'Type of the wise who soar but never roam;
True to the kindred points of heaven and home!'

are examples that come to mind akin to what the Japanese were able to read into the *kachō-e* of the masters.

Certain of the very greatest of the Kanō and other classical schools are revered for their *kachō-e*. Sesshū in the fifteenth century, Utanosuke and Sōtan in the sixteenth, Kōetsu, Sōtatsu, Kōrin Hōitsu, Sosen, Ōkyo and Ganku in the seventeenth and eighteenth centuries, are a few of the artists whose names are illustrious for their work in this genre, and among whose paintings it is true to say that there are some of the greatest flower and animal paintings in the world. Such paintings are on a completely different plane from those of most Western artists using similar subjects and point to one of the fundamental distinctions between the painting of the two hemispheres, a distinction that can be applied generally and not merely to the type of painting under discussion.

Of European paintings of animals and of plants, omitting those of professed scientific purpose such as the illustrations to botanical and ornithological works, it is clear that the flower-pieces of Huysum, Fantin-Latour or Brabazon, and the animal studies of Dürer and Landseer—to take a typical group—were painted with one overriding aim: a desire to give as literal a representation of the object depicted as the medium allowed. We clap our hands at the dewdrop on the leaves, the separate single hairs of the rabbit's fur, the dazzling whiteness of the camellias in the sunshine: the artist has mimicked nature so deceptively. But the oriental artists had no such restricted aim as mere imitation: they did not normally 'draw from nature', but stored the images in the mind until the mood was upon them to paint, until there was that 'spontaneous overflow of powerful feelings' from an 'emotion recollected in tranquillity'.

Thus unhampered by the tyranny of 'representation', they not only imbued their work with the undertones of their own personalities, but were left free to develop a special genius innate in them, it would seem, for the line, the arabesque, the pattern, the fitting of a design to a given space with a sort of inevitability. With us, the felicities of composition and pattern have been achieved in spite of our method; they are often the result of chance, not of design.

The oriental gift for spacing and for patterning could not have been realized with the 'naturalistic' technique of the occident. Modelling 'in the round', lights and shadows, and perspective as a matter of 'parallel lines vanishing to a point on the horizon' were avoided by the Japanese, and it is the resultant flatness and formal arrangement of natural objects that comes as one of the obstacles to our initial approach to far-eastern art. It was not, as some have hastily assumed, an inability on the part of the Japanese to draw 'in the round': it was simply not their method. Yet their portrayal of natural forms was invariably convincing—they reproduced the 'very life', as Utamaro did of the world of insects.

In the past, artists of the Ukiyo-e school had pitted their skill against the masters of the Kanō in the field of *kachō-e*. Kiyomasu and Shigenaga, in the early decades of the eighteenth century, produced some hand-coloured woodcuts of predatory birds that are the very soul of rapaciousness; a famous print by Harunobu is of a vase of flowers drenched in the light of the moon that rises full-

26. *Cicada and spider on sweet-corn.* From the *Insect Book*. 1788.

faced over them; Koryūsai made most poetic compositions of birds and flowers; and other cases could be instanced of artists seeming to choose their subjects in a desire to add stature to the Ukiyo-e school, and clear the imputation of superficiality and commonness.

Yet even in choosing his particular subjects, Utamaro showed that strain of originality, of whimsicality, which is so pronounced in him. The title of a Japanese book is rarely to be taken at its face value merely, and in the prints of Utamaro's *Selected Insects* the greater emphasis is far oftener on the fruits and flowers than the insects: but even so, the insect had never before received the attention given to the rest of the animate world. Utamaro was the first to use them as Utanosuke used the eagle or Sō-ami the tiger. There is nothing scientific, of course, in the selection (indeed, a spider, a snake, a lizard and a frog all figure as 'insects'), but it was something novel in a picture-book to have a series of prints with a theme like this; and that it proved popular may, I think, be

deduced from the fact that Utamaro followed it up with two further books of prints with connecting themes—the *Shell Book*, and the '*Hundred Screamers*' or *Bird Book*.

As for the prints, nothing more exquisite in the way of engraving and printing had been seen before. They, and those of the *Shell* and *Bird* books, represent the *ne plus ultra* of colour-print technique. The subtlest shades in every possible gradation, the micaceous sheen on the wings, the iridescence of the snail-shell, the hair-fine lines of antennae and minute limbs, are reproduced from Utamaro's drawings with a meticulous delicacy.

Each design extends over a double-page as the book is opened out. The verse, in graceful, flowing *hiragana*, an adornment in itself, takes its place in each composition. There is no attempt completely to fill the pages, the design demands a concentration here, a blank page there, and it is just this feeling for perfect spacing that constitutes one of the especial beauties of the prints, and one the least translatable into words.

CHAPTER SEVEN

THE ALBUMS OF PRINTS
1788–1790

WE HAVE NO MEANS of telling what effect the *Insect Book* had on the Edo public, though it is perhaps significant that it was sufficiently well-liked for another edition to be called for as late as 1823, when, under a new title, the prints appeared, so badly printed and in colours so vile that they are a travesty of those of the first issue. Copies of the 1788 edition are rare, but sufficient numbers have survived to prove it must have been a treasured book, a *de luxe* novelty that probably brought Utamaro into real prominence for the first time, especially with a clientele who were likely to embolden him to fresh exploits in the realm of the coloured picture-book and in other untried directions.

Certainly, the period immediately following 1788 is one of immense productivity, during which his exertions finally established him as the most potent force in the Ukiyo-e school and led directly to the boldest innovations in the nineties. There is a persistent tradition that Kiyonaga's retirement from print-making, he who for a decade had been the undisputed leader of the school, was due to his having been ousted from his position about 1790 by an all-conquering Utamaro. There is no need to believe this, indeed it is a most unlikely story, but in it may be some grain of truth relating to Utamaro's sudden conquest of the public at this time.

Four albums were published by Tsutajū at short intervals about this time, each containing five prints most elaborately printed: *Ehon Waka Ebisu* ('*Young God Ebisu*', i.e. '*New Year's Festival*'), undated but probably 1788; *Ehon Kyōgetsubō* ('*The Moon-mad Monk*'), 1789; *Ehon Gin Sekai* ('*The Silver World*'), and *Fugen-zō* ('*The Image of Fugen*' or '*Fugen Blossoms*'), both in 1790. These albums form a natural group as they have other factors in common apart from their format. In 1788 appeared, too, the finest of the coloured erotic books, *Uta-makura*, ('*The Poem of the Pillow*'); in 1790, or the next year, the *Shell Book* and the *Bird Book*; about 1792, the wonderful series of half-length portraits on mica

backgrounds; and throughout these three or four years, a number of smaller books in black and white (some of which have been mentioned already in Chapter IV), including a considerable group of *kibyōshi*. Then there are the separate sheet prints, though there are few apart from the half-length portraits and a few triptychs mentioned later in this chapter that can be ascribed to the period. When it is considered that Utamaro was also executing brush paintings in this period in addition to designing for the prints and *ehon*, his fecundity and industry will be apparent.

Each of the albums now to be described was inspired by a different theme: *Waka Ebisu* by the New Year's Day; *Kyōgetsubō* by the moon; *Gin Sekai* by the snow; and *Fugen-zō* by the flowering trees of spring-time; and Utamaro is throughout engrossed with the beauty of the world around, this time with open-air landscape scenes rather than the minutiae that had filled the pages of the *Insect Book*: yet, as can be seen from the themes inspiring these new volumes, the underlying motif is 'Snow, Moon and Flowers', *Setsugekka*, only another classical variant of *kachō-e*, typifying the beauties of nature.

They are printed in a singularly precious way with much use of gold for conventional cloud forms (an artifice common to the Tosa School but hardly ever employed by Utamaro outside these albums), and are among the most delightful of all Utamaro's works. In them appear some of his finest landscapes. Moreover, the prints are essentially Japanese; the festivals they depict, the evident worship of the snow and moon and the flowering trees, whilst giving the prints supremely lovely subjects, also bear witness to that engaging and deep-seated Japanese trait discussed above and called, for want of a better word, 'nature-worship'.

The first of the four is probably *Waka Ebisu*, consisting of scenes of New Year's Day celebrations, with humorous poems for the occasion (Pl. IV). It is undated, but on internal evidence seems to belong to 1788. (The monkey appearing in the last print

27. *A faggot-gatherer crossing a bridge over a waterfall.* From the album *The Moon-mad Monk.* 1789.

28. *Monochrome landscape*, from the album *The Silver World.* 1790.

may be an allusion to the Year of the Monkey, which fell in 1788[1]).

In Japan, New Year's Day is celebrated, as in some European countries, with holiday festivals, dancing, exchange of gifts, and a great number of picturesque ceremonies, many of which have become familiar to us through the prints. The extraordinary thing about two of the five prints in this album is that they have evidently been designed in a purposely archaic manner, just as in our depiction of Christmas scenes we continue to hark back to the past and draw coaches and horses, half-timbered inns and snow-covered villages, all in an early Victorian manner. One is an exercise in the Tosa style, the other is modelled on Moronobu— perhaps in homage to the first great master of Ukiyo-e.

The *Picture-Book of the Moon-mad Monk* is actually a series of illustrations to humorous poems relating to the moon, but in effect is a set of 'landscapes with figures' with the full moon as the connecting link between them. Some of these are not what one would call 'typical' of Utamaro's work, even of this period—there is again that odd flirting with the Tosa style, though assuredly only in fun; one landscape is in pseudo-Kanō style, and the last plate has Chinese tendencies; but even apart from this variety of styles that prevents any sense of oneness about the prints, those in Ukiyo-e style are untypical. Perhaps in this period of transition, before the influences of his earlier models had been entirely thrown off, Utamaro was trying his hand in a number of styles.

One convention that will be noted in all the prints, for it is characteristic of Japanese painting generally, is the indication that it is night-time, not as we do by draining the picture of colour and covering everything, veritably, under the cloak of darkness (the most perfect picture of night on these terms would be a completely inky canvas on which all forms are lost), but simply by some tell-tale feature which, like the placards announcing a scene in the Elizabethan theatre, tells the onlooker that it is night-time: the moon, lanterns, a link-boy with a flaming brand. Sometimes the sky is actually darkened, but even then the colours of dresses and the features of faces are as bright and as clearly defined as in the light of day. That is not to say that no attempt is made to give the atmosphere of a moonlight night, for example, but this is achieved in a manner quite different from our own. To take the first plate of the *Moon-mad Monk*, we find that a most exquisite rendering of the luminosity of the moonlit sky is achieved by the contrast of the brilliantly coloured dresses of the bevy of girls foregathered, with a young man, on the verandah of a house of refreshment, with the pale greyish tones of the world outside. The moon is seen rising above the distant house-tops dim in the dusk, and as ever with the Japanese artists, is invested with a magic of its own.

The most remarkable print in this album is an

29. *In the grounds of a tea-house.* Triptych. About 1786–8.

[1] A copy of the book has now come to light that has a printed date at the end of the colophon, viz. *tori no hatsuharu*, 'early spring in the year of the cock', which corresponds to 1789.

essay in the Kanō style. It is in monochrome, has a typical rocky landscape with a waterfall as its subject, and the brushstrokes are unmistakably those learned so laboriously in the exacting school known by the family name of its sixteenth-century founders (Fig. 27). The two figures crossing the bridge over the waterfall and silhouetted against the great globe of the full moon are entirely subordinated to the landscape: as ever in the finest Kanō painting, one senses the insignificance of man against the vastness of natural forms and forces. It would be idle to claim for Utamaro's essay the majesty of Motonobu or the power of Tanyū but it is by no means inconsiderable in its own right, and shows, too, as in other works at this time, the 'Insect Book' above all, a high-minded seriousness and a desire to contend

for honours even with the greatest.

Snow, the theme of another album, has always had a high place in the Japanese pantheon of nature-worship, and has, like the flowers and birds, been depicted with an almost holy passion by artists of all schools. Perhaps its wonderfully decorative effect—the limning of a white line on the bamboos' and pine trees' green, the stippling of the grey sky with white flakes unevenly and yet in perfect pattern like their own decorative designs—has something to do with their love for it. The exclamation of a Japanese servant-girl, translated in de Goncourt's book, shows how even the humbler people felt when confronted by the beauty of the snow and its pattern: 'Oh I entreat you,' she cries, 'do not send me out to market today, madame,

30. *Children playing in the snow*, from the album *The Silver World*. 1790.

the little dog had flowered all the courtyard with his pads. I would not wish to blot out such delicate patterns.' In *The Silver World* the bright colours of trees and house interiors are intensified by being set against the dazzling whiteness of the snow. And how wonderfully the snow is depicted, and the tingling air, the still sky—as you look through this album you almost expect to breathe out white vapour, the chill atmosphere is so wonderfully suggested. One of the landscapes, a boat on a river with people promenading on the bank, is perhaps less convincing than the others—one is forced to admit that in some of Hiroshige's landscapes this same sort of thing is done so much more successfully; but who, before Utamaro, had achieved so much in the realm of pure landscape as he did? Not even Hiroshige, whose snow scenes are among his finest works, produced a more desolate wintry scene than that depicted in another print in this album, in which the effect is obtained entirely by gradated blacks and greys (Fig. 28). This is an exquisite double page, and the use of bygone conventions—for the style is that of the early landscape masters—produces an uncanny effect of cold, of drear December. Another memorable print in this album shows

children at play in the snow (Fig. 30), with a peculiar brightness, a preciousness in the colouring that irresistibly recalls an earlier master, Harunobu.

Fugen-zō follows this book as spring follows winter (the prefaces to these two albums were written in February and April 1790, respectively). The literal translation of the title is '*The Image of Fugen*',[1] Fugen being a Buddhist deity and traditionally the personification of sagacity, though as Utamaro has depicted in these fine prints the gaiety and irresponsibility of youth in the spring-tide of life, some irony appears to be intended in the title. The first print shows a group of girls watching from a balcony a procession that is passing down the main street of the Yoshiwara, but the avenue of cherry-trees is in flower, and all they can see through the cloud of pink blossom is the blue umbrella-tops of passers-by. Another is of a picnic party held in a clearing in the flowering woods, a group of men awaiting the arrival of an approaching procession of girls. And the next shows the dire consequences of this picnic, where the *sake*-cup was plied too often. The party of girls wends its way home and one of them, palpably the worse for drink, is being

[1] The name also of a species of cherry-tree.

31. *Girls watching awabi divers at Enoshima*. From a triptych. About 1789.

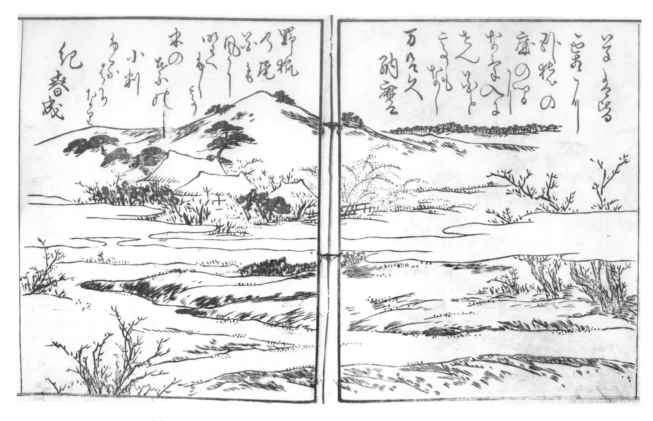

32. *A hamlet in the hills*, from the picture-book *The Island of Artemesia*. 1790.

assisted along by two of her companions. The men can be seen following behind. The colour in this plate is itself heady like wine, and suggests the very perfume of the spring flowers (cf. Pl. V).

There is a sort of untroubled happiness, the lavish gold in the clouds is hardly needed to tell that these are the pictures of a Golden Age. They are, too, among the finest of Utamaro's landscapes —Koechlin (who wrote a notable preface to the *Paris Catalogue*) thinks they are his best, and points out that he led the way for the great land-scapists of the Popular School, Masayoshi, Hokusai and Hiroshige.

Koechlin refers also to another book of this same year 1790, called *Ehon Yomoghi no Chima* ('*The Island of Artemesia*') with over forty illustrations, mainly landscape, in black and white. Koechlin says that the Popular School 'had never before given such faithful pictures of the Japanese country-side as these valleys, these flowering woods and these rivers; Hokusai must have studied books such as this'. But this seems an excessive claim for the rather slight drawings in this book (Fig. 32).

To the years that saw the publication of the four notable albums, a small number of separate *nishiki-e* can be attributed. Principal among these are two triptychs, one of *Girls watching awabi divers at Enoshima* (Fig. 31), the other of *Holiday-makers fishing with rod and line at Enoshima*.

There is an assurance, an accomplishment, in both these prints that bespeaks the master. We begin to observe a change in the figures of the women. Hitherto, especially in the books and albums described above, Utamaro had shown a predilection for those of short stature with rounded heads, with little suggestion, for all their grace, of the fashionably tall women familiar to us from the later prints. Koechlin noted that in the *Island of Artemesia* there was an elongation of form, a more oval face, and in these two triptychs there is a new note of elegance which, though still recalling Kiyonaga, has begun to move away from his ideal. But what one principally notices about these trip-tychs, and the equally charming triptych repro-duced (Fig. 29), is a 'freshness and sweetness that is quite delicious'. And Binyon and Sexton, using those words, continue: 'The Kiyonaga types are here, and the outdoor scene, the sense of fresh air, the landscape setting, are what Kiyonaga had brought into Ukiyo-ye. But again, as before, there is very perceptible that genius for design, for relating figures and groups to one another with natural felicity and freshness, in which Utamaro was to excel all his compeers, his predecessors and successors; and with that a buoyancy, a playfulness, a sweetness, such as had hardly appeared in Ukiyo-ye since Harunobu.'

With all the rich harvest of these years, and of earlier years too, it seems singularly ungracious on Fenollosa's part to attempt to deprive Utamaro of the admiration due to him simply because the later work, better known, is more 'typically' Utamaro, and, to Fenollosa, decadent. Kiyonaga was, for Fenollosa, the 'culmination of the culmination', and for Utamaro, as the scapegoat for the decadence in Ukiyo-e art, his praise is ever grudging, or faint and damning. 'It is vain', he wrote, 'for the admirers of Utamaro to rank him chiefly for his work in Temmei (1781–1788). That which is most Utamaro-ish in Utamaro is a new art, one which

appears to a new populace, an art of a new age, whose coarser habit of mind stimulates a powerful but coarser genius.'[1]

Even if this last statement were accepted, with its implied criticism of the later works, surely, in those early years, as I have tried to show, Utamaro had produced sufficient works to be accounted among the elect. Whatever the assessment of the later prints, they need not cause us to amend judgment on the earlier: in arriving at an estimate of Blake's poetry, we do not dismiss the *Songs of Innocence* because of the unintelligibility of the Prophetic Books that came afterwards, nor do we scruple to prefer Whistler's *Thames Set* etchings even though the artist employed a different technique, by which he himself set more store, in the Venice sets of later years. It is almost symptomatic of greatness in an artist that there should be a continual development throughout his career, a constant striving for new, more adequate forms of expression. We can enjoy the best of both worlds, the spontaneous freshness of early manhood, the studied extravagances of maturity: and if Utamaro is to be 'ranked' at all (and it seems a profitless pastime) it would be unjust to ignore either the one or the other.

[1]'The Masters of Ukiyo-ye' (Catalogue of an Exhibition held in New York in 1896).

CHAPTER EIGHT

THE JAPANESE COURTESAN

JUST WHY the courtesan always proved so popular a subject with the colour-print artists has always been a matter of curiosity to us. We can understand the popularity of pictures of noted actors in their favourite roles since theatrical prints recorded actual stage performances, and as mementoes of visits to the theatres and as representations of the players, who were idolized with all the fervour now accorded to film stars in America, a ready public was assured. But although 'public' figures, it is hard to imagine the courtesans having the following of the fêted actor, and in any case, depictions of them were never 'portraits' in our sense of the term, never the likenesses of individuals, even though their names were usually inscribed on the prints.

In many cases, they seem to have been introduced to display to best advantage fashionable dresses, as noted mannequins exhibit the creations of dress designers in the West. The courtesans were always clad in the height of fashion, and to a nation so intent upon the refinements of dress—of men and women alike—this type of print had its interest as a fashion-plate: indeed, some prints by Utamaro are professed advertisements for famous houses of fashion.

But there were stronger reasons than that behind the popularity of this order of prints. They depicted not merely the courtesans in their fine array, but also their environment, the 'Green Houses' of the Yoshiwara, the ritualistic life of the denizens, the clandestine comings and goings, the festivals and the promenades: all ministering to what must have been an insatiable curiosity of the Edo citizens concerning this little world within a world. Most men aspired unashamedly to the pleasures the Yoshiwara held out. If they could afford to gratify their aspirations, the colour-prints were a constant reminder of their pleasure; or, if they could not, the prints enabled them to enjoy the company of the courtesans vicariously.

Up to about 1792, the courtesan and her quarters had not figured more in Utamaro's work than they did in that of any other artist of the Ukiyo-e school. As time went on, however, Utamaro devoted more and more attention to the 'violets' and their attendants, and to the daily round of the Green Houses, until in the end they claimed him entirely. This obsession is one of the keys both to Utamaro's work and to the legends of his profligacy, and some consideration of the courtesan as an element in Edo life becomes necessary.

It is safe to say, I think, that concerning no other Japanese phenomenon has there been so much misunderstanding, so many conflicting views, from the one extreme that the Yoshiwara was a vile institution and its votaries 'lost' women, to the other that no stigma attached to the profession, and that in some cases it was not without honour.

Most of the difficulties we have in arriving at a just estimate are due to our natural tendencies to look at Japanese social life from the Western viewpoint and, in this case, to see no difference between the Yoshiwara and the Western brothel, or between the *oiran* and common prostitutes. But from antiquity (as any reader of Arthur Waley's lovely translation of the Genji Romance will agree), the Japanese view of promiscuity has differed from our own, the taint of immorality is far weaker than to us. In Europe there are things that are deemed immoral that elsewhere are quite customary. Monogamy is preached as part of the Christian religion, but not of the Mohammedan; whilst it is not thought immoral for the Arab to have two or more wives, in the West it is a criminal offence. It is obviously wrong to pass judgment on the licensing of prostitution, or institutions like the Yoshiwara, after applying the ethics and laws of the West; they must be assessed on the canons prevailing in Japan. It is quite legitimate to compare the systems and standards of Japan on the one hand and of this country on the other, and to decide that in our view the Eastern code is less moral than our own, but it is another thing to charge the Japanese with immorality when they were merely following the allowed practices of their own country. With equal justice, we might be accused of cowardice by the Japanese because we do not commit *hara-kiri* when their code of honour would demand it.

In Japan, the Yoshiwara may not have been looked upon as an wholly innocent diversion for young men: but, because of the entirely different sense of moral values prevailing, we should be careful to distinguish it from the apparently similar institutions of London and Paris.

Another factor that has stood in the way of a just appreciation of this issue is that so much of our knowledge of the Japanese way of life is derived not from native writers but from Europeans, who knew the country only after it had been opened up to foreign influences and had suffered changes almost wholly evil since Utamaro's day. Already, indeed, before the advent of Commander Perry in 1853, disruptive elements had been at work within the social structure; the nature of the Japanese people, the so-called common people, the patrons of the print-designers, whose love of beauty and formal pattern, of colour and poetry, was innate, had coarsened and become vulgarized. The pleasures of the Japanese people with whom Europeans and Americans first made contact were already not those of their forerunners of one hundred or even fifty years earlier. And yet it is on the eye-witness accounts of this altered Japan that attempts are made to reconstruct the world of the colour-print artists of the eighteenth century, which might be likened to a Japanese attempting to write of pre-revolution France on what he saw in Paris in the 1850s.

Some of the most sympathetic descriptions of this later Japan are to be found interspersed among the *Tales of Old Japan* written by A. B. Mitford (later Lord Redesdale) in the sixties of the last century. Due allowance must be made for the sixty years that had elapsed since Utamaro's death and for the fact that Mitford wrote for a Victorian audience; all the same, his information about the Yoshiwara is enlightening and factual, and makes a most effective contrast to the persuasive propaganda of de Goncourt, and to the rhapsodies of Jippensha Ikku in a famous book, illustrated by Utamaro, the *Seirō Ehon Nenjū Gyōji* of 1804, described in Chapter XIX.

He begins with an historical sketch of the origins of the Yoshiwara: how, in 1617, the various brothels scattered about Edo were concentrated in one place at Fukiyachō called Yoshiwara (meaning the 'rush-moor', though by use of an alternative character with the same sound *yoshi* it came to have

33. *Anxious in Love*, from a set *Chosen Poems*. About 1791–2.

the significance 'lucky moor'); and how later, in 1655, when Edo was beginning to increase in size and importance, the Yoshiwara was moved bodily to the northern part of the town, whilst still preserving its old name. As some indication of its size in 1869, he quotes a return of that year listing 153 brothels, containing 3,289 courtesans of all classes, 'from the *Oiran*, or proud beauty, who, dressed up in gorgeous brocades of gold and silver, with painted face and gilded lips, and with her teeth fashionably blacked, has all the young bloods of Yedo at her feet, down to the humblest *Shinzo*, or white-toothed woman, who rots away her life in the common stews'.

Of the manner in which women were recruited for the Yoshiwara he writes: 'Courtesans, singing women, and dancers are bought by contractors either as children, when they are educated for their calling, or at a more advanced age when their

34. *The unwilling lover*. Diptych. About 1794.

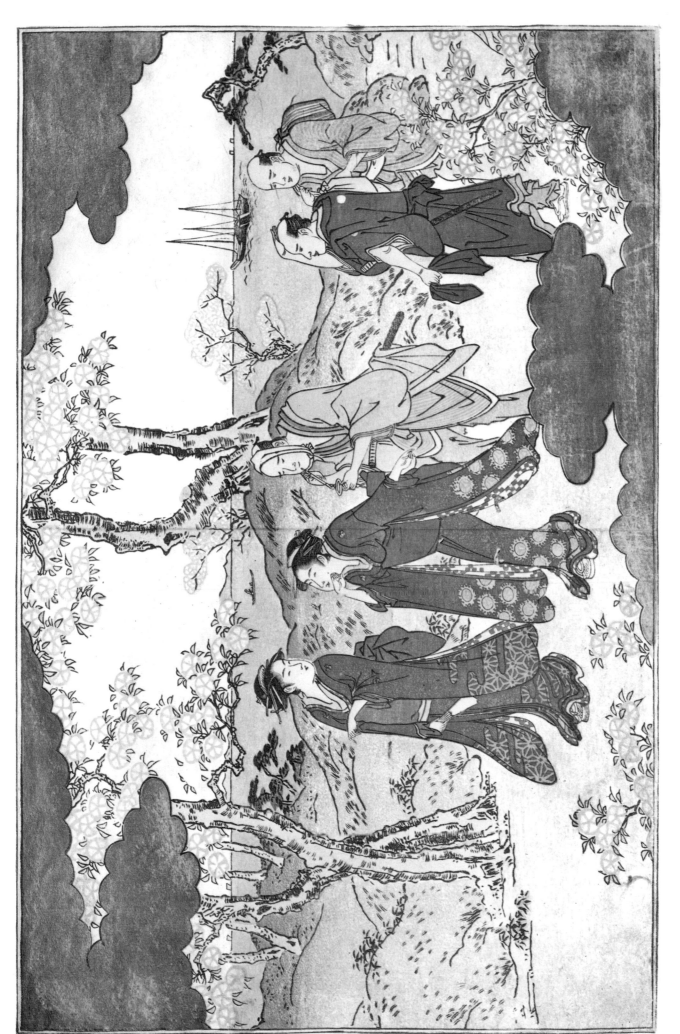

V. *A cherry-blossom-viewing party*, from *The Image of Fugen*. 1790.

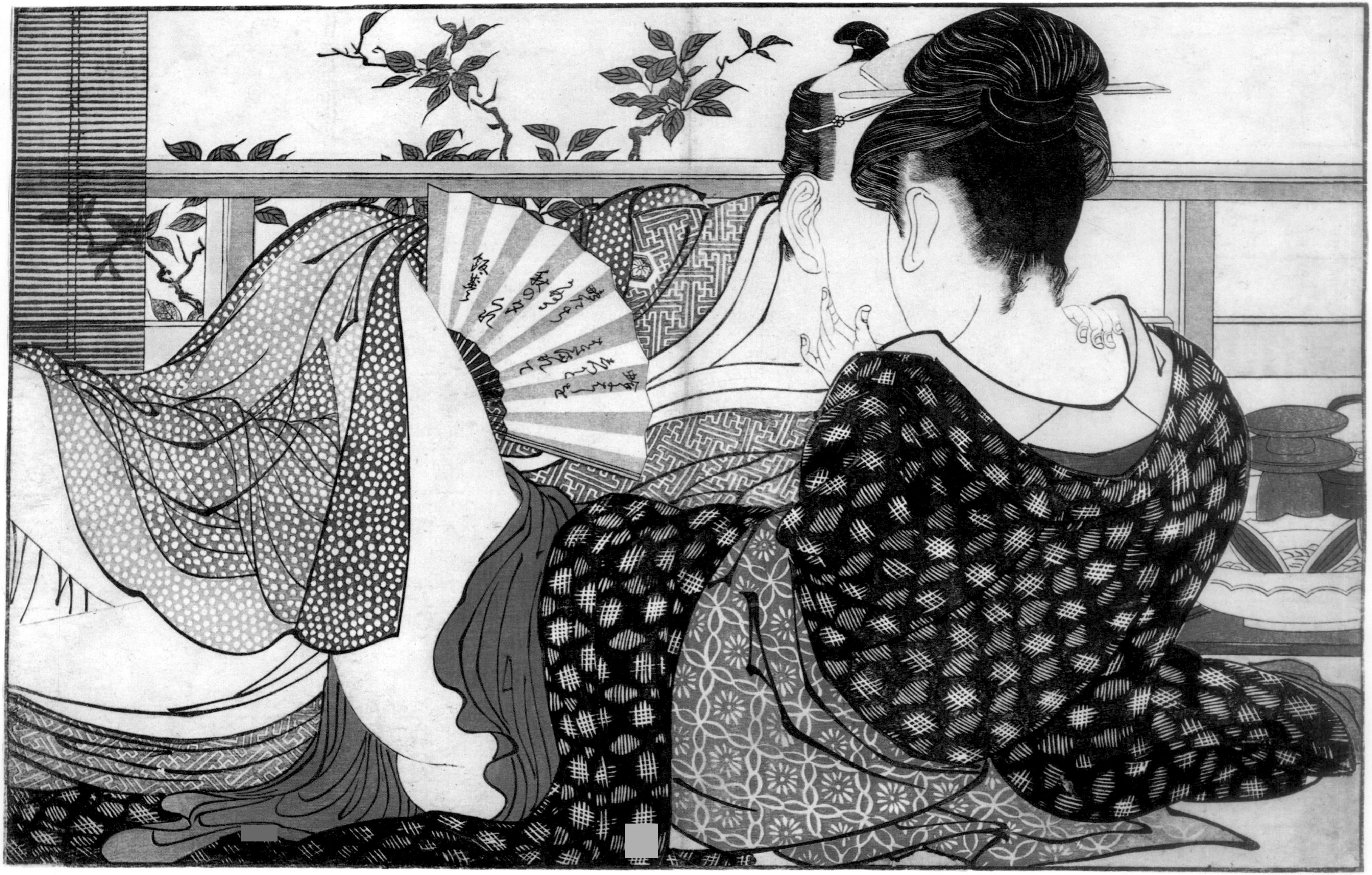

VI. *Lovers*, from *The Poem of the Pillow*. 1788.

accomplishments and charms render them desirable investments. The engagement is never made life-long, for once past the flower of their youth the poor creatures would be mere burthens upon their masters; a courtesan is usually bought until she shall have reached the age of twenty-seven, after which she becomes her own property. Singers remain longer in harness, but even they rarely work after the age of thirty, for Japanese women, like Italians, age quickly, and have none of that intermediate stage between youth and old age, which seems to be confined to countries where there is a twilight.'

'Little children who are bought for purposes of prostitution at the age of five or six years fetch about the same price as those that are bought to be singers. During their novitiate they are employed to wait upon the *oiran*, or fashionable courtesans, in the capacity of little female pages (*kamuro*). They are mostly the children of distressed persons, or orphans whom their relatives cruelly sell rather than be at the expense and trouble of bringing them up. Of the girls who enter the profession later in life, some are orphans, who have no other means of earning a livelihood; others sell their bodies out of filial piety, that they may succour their sick or needy parents; others are married women who enter the Yoshiwara to supply the wants of their husbands; and a very small proportion is recruited from girls who have been seduced and abandoned, perhaps sold by faithless lovers.'

'The time to see the Yoshiwara to the best advantage is just after nightfall, when the lamps are lighted. Then it is that the women—who for the last two hours have been engaged in gilding their lips and painting their eyebrows black, and their throats and bosoms a snowy white, carefully leaving three brown Vandyke collar points where the back of the head joins the neck, in accordance with one of the strictest rules in Japanese cosmetic science—leave the back rooms and take their places side by side, in a kind of long narrow cage, the wooden bars of which open on to the public thoroughfare.'

'Here they sit for hours, gorgeous in dresses of silk and gold and silver embroidery, speechless and motionless as wax figures, until they shall have attracted the attention of some of the passers-by who begin to throng the place.'

In another passage the writer deals with the moral issues involved, though he draws no distinction between courtesan of Japan and the hostess of the *maison close*. Probably by his time the gap between the two had to some extent closed:

'I have heard it stated, and seen it printed, that it is no disgrace for a respectable Japanese to sell his daughter, that men of position and family often choose their wives from such places as 'The Three Sea-coasts' and that up to the time of her marriage the conduct of a young girl is a matter of no importance whatever. Nothing could be more unjust or more untrue. It is only the neediest people that sell their children to be waitresses, singers and prostitutes. It does occasionally happen that the daughter of a *samurai*, or gentleman, is found in a house of ill-fame, but such a case could only occur at the death or utter ruin of the parents, and an official investigation of the matter has proved it to be so exceptional, that the presence of a young lady in such a place is an enormous attraction, her superior education and accomplishments shedding a lustre over the house. . . . And yet a girl is not disgraced if for her parents' sake she sells herself to a life of misery so great that when a Japanese enters a house of ill-fame, he is forced to leave his sword and dirk at the door for two reasons—first to prevent brawling; secondly, because it is known that some of the women inside so loathe their existence that they would put an end to it, could they get hold of a weapon.'

These are the sordid facts elicited by a careful investigator of the 1860s, set down with the same condemnatory intention as he would have had in exposing the vice of Soho or Montmartre. Edmond de Goncourt, with less prejudice on this issue than the worthy Englishman, and aided too, as he acknowledges, by his Japanese dragoman, Hayashi, gives a different picture.

'Europe', he says, writing in 1891, 'has very wrong ideas of Japanese prostitution, *at least of the prostitution of the last century and the early part of the present century*. The fifty "Green Houses" of the Yoshiwara and the hundreds outside the barrier, owed their gorgeous existence, their splendour, not to the rich population of Edo, nor to strangers, but to the ambassadors, the *chargés d'affaires* of the three-hundred-and-sixty Princes attached to the Shogun and living in the capital without their families. Thus the woman of the "Green House" was not the low prostitute imagined from knowledge of our own prostitutes, the woman enjoyed as soon as the

35. *A courtesan dreaming of her wedding*. About 1798–1800.
(The inset, a classic subject of which the print is an analogue, shows Rosei, a Chinese scholar,
who slept on a magic pillow, dreaming of wonderful, but never realized, happenings.)

36. *A sake party*. About 1796–8.
(The silhouettes of the girl's companions are seen through the semi-transparent *shōji* [sliding partition].)

threshold is passed, the woman without class. . . . The woman of the "Green Houses" is the Courtesan.'

The author of the text of the *Annals of the Green Houses*, Jippensha Ikku, was a well-known writer and artist who was probably as familiar with the world of the courtesan as Utamaro himself, and whose picture, allowing always for the heightening of colour usual with Japanese writers of this type of literature, can be trusted. He says:

'The girls of the Yoshiwara are brought up like princesses from infancy, they are given the most complete education. They are taught reading, writing, all about music and art and the "tea" and "perfume" ceremonies. They are just like princesses educated at the Palace—then why look askance at an outlay of 1000 ryōs?'

From Ikku and other sources we learn that the language the novitiate courtesans were taught was not that of every day, but the classical language, the language of the Court and its poetry between the seventh and tenth centuries. The grand courtesan, the consort of nobles and court officials, was called a *tayū* or *oiran*. Under her she had two young girls called *kamuro* who began as her attendants (often depicted in the prints in dresses of a pattern identical with the courtesan's, as if it were a livery), and who would later become *shinzō*, that is, courtesans of a lower order. Depending on whether her charms, or her ability to profit by the grooming of the exacting regime, warranted the promotion, a *shinzō* might eventually graduate as an *oiran*.

The courtesan was not to be hired against her will, nor did *le contact des deux épidermes* ensue immediately; there were formalities in the relationship between the courtesan and her lover, she had to be wooed, and three visits, with their prescribed ceremonial, were indispensable before there was intimacy. It is these ceremonies that figure so largely in the prints and form the major part of the *Annals of the Green Houses*. The first visit was no more than a formal introduction; the second a repetition of the first, with the granting of as many of those additional favours as etiquette sanctioned; and on the third visit, the stranger might attain to what was called 'full knowledge'.

Even among the *tayū* and *oiran* (the principal courtesans) there were degrees of rank, pride of place going to those who made up the 'Grand Promenade'. The courtesan of the prints of such artists as Kiyonaga, Eishi and Utamaro is the aristocrat, the princess of her calling, a personage of the utmost refinement, queenly in bearing, wearing her splendid apparel with the assurance of a trained model. Her days were passed in ceremony, or preparations for ceremony: within the precincts of the Yoshiwara, as we know from so many artists' pictures, Utamaro's above all, affairs were ordered with the strict etiquette of an exacting court. Her amusements were those of the nobility: the games, the music, the composing of poetry, the handwriting and painting competitions.

Outside of the *shunga*, we are never made aware of the 'business' side of these houses, and it is rare for the courtesans to be shown in any relationship with men that could be called the least bit compromising. As in the *Annals of the Green Houses*, the intrigues, the flirtations, the quite unexceptional proceedings of the first meetings, are portrayed, but never more.

As for the women themselves, we can only conjecture what their true feelings were. Like the bird reared in a cage—a symbol of their own captivity that often accompanies their portraits—in most cases they had never known the doubtful freedom other women enjoyed, and for perhaps that reason accepted their lot uncomplainingly. Their way of life was not considered, as I have tried to show, as shameful as it is in Europe, they had freedom of choice of their paramours, exercised their domination with the jealousy of kept mistresses, and within the little world of the Yoshiwara were treated as persons of consequence, surrounded by the luxury of fine silks, expensive perfumes and all the rich trappings of their calling: to many such girls, taken as children from impoverished homes, this may have seemed world enough. But that there were those that suffered, if not under a sense of shame then something akin to it, we gather from the sigh we occasionally overhear recorded, accidentally almost, in the writings of the time, and sometimes, even unintentionally, Utamaro has given a look of wistful resignation to his lovely women more eloquent than open rebellion.

CHAPTER NINE

'THE POEM OF THE PILLOW'

IT IS NECESSARY to go back a little now, to 1788, the date of the publication of *Uta-makura* ('*The Poem of the Pillow*'), acknowledged to be the finest of the erotic albums with colour-prints. There is a natural tendency upon the part of writers on Japanese artists to pass over in silence books that are often to our eyes repellent, but they formed so large and important a part of the *œuvre* of some artists (and in Utamaro's case contain some astonishing tours-de-force) that only a partial impression of an artist's output is given if all mention of this type of work is omitted.

Of necessity they are the least known of Utamaro's works, and the passing references to them in books are veiled allusions that do no more than pique curiosity, the reader being left in doubt whether such prints are, in fact, so outrageous, so utterly beyond the pale, as the authorities imply. Are they, as Strange says, 'quite beyond all European canons of good taste', or is it a case of Western prudery holding up its hands in horror at some trifling indecencies? It can be admitted at once that, however broadminded one attempts to be when looking at them, the majority come as a shock. Depictions of the physical act follow page after page, with the utmost realism, verging often on the macabre and the grotesque, and with all the variations suggested by lubricity and a fertile brush.

And yet, Strange is one of those who admit that these books contain some of Utamaro's best work, they show to a marked degree his splendid faculty for composition and colour, the very demands of his subject impelling him to surprising shifts in the arrangement of two figures upon a page. They give one an opportunity, rare elsewhere, to assess Utamaro's undoubted power in the drawing of the human figure, so often with him only the vehicle for gracefully exhibiting a lovely dress. On this there are no two voices. Arthur Morrison wrote: 'Certain nude figures in some of Utamaro's pictures seem to be Greek, rather than Japanese. It is difficult to present examples, for on the rare occasions on which the Japanese drew the nude they did it with a frank simplicity that might shock the nerves of persons who enjoy the blessings of our not very frank

and not very simple civilisation: in other words, the Japanese of a century ago had not invented the fig-leaf; an engine of manners which even the Japanese of today first encounters with emotion not so much of admiration as of stupefaction.'

Some have asked how could a master of Utamaro's known refinement of artistry (the *Ehon Waka Ebisu*, for instance, was published about the same time as '*The Poem of the Pillow*'), how could he, with his often-expressed pride in his calling, come to produce what we are inclined to look upon as crudely pornographic prints? Are they not just another proof of the wantonness, the profligacy, that tradition ascribes to him?

As with other aspects of Japanese art that puzzle us, any attempt at an understanding can only be successful if we try first to move away from the Western standpoint to one nearer the Japanese. Just as it is inaccurate to take the European brothel as a parallel to the Yoshiwara, so would it be unwise to condemn the erotic art of the Ukiyo-e on the same grounds as we condemn that of Western artists. Where a different moral code exists, where nations are nearer to or further from the natural man, where the respective civilizations are, going back to Morrison, more or less 'frank' in matters of sex, the view in which erotic art is held will vary. Certainly, I think it must be conceded that it is unjust to condemn these pictures as immoral or indecent simply because by our canons they are so. What may be unexceptionable in one country at one period may be reprehensible in another country at a different period. Everyone is familiar with Rembrandt's painting in the National Gallery of a little girl paddling. I well remember my sense of disillusionment—I was young at the time—when I read Mr Wilenski's book on Dutch painting and learned that this little girl, who, I had thought, was sensibly holding up her skirt to her knees to prevent it getting wet, was, in the eyes of the Dutch people of the seventeenth century, committing an act of the most outrageous eroticism. The ground positively opened beneath me. A thousand grotesque possibilities began to suggest themselves for pictures that I had hitherto regarded as irreproachably innocent in motive. The lesson was a salutary one, in that it emphasized the fallacy of judging the attitude to sex of a foreign people by standards prevailing here and now. Even the erogenous zones vary with time and geographical situation; the knees aroused the libido in Holland in the seventeenth century, the nape of the neck in Japan in the eighteenth, and the whole matter is as much a biological one as the factors determining the colour of each race's skin.

In considering the Japanese people, too, the margin of error in our judgment may be still further increased because it has been no part of their religion, as it has been of Christianity, to lay an imputation of sin on sex. In a country where phallicism was an openly professed cult, and where procreation, rather than romantic love, was the be-all and end-all of marriage, and where too, as Morrison remarked, they had not invented the fig-leaf, the depiction of the physical act may have given rise to little sense of shame or shock. That it brings both to us should not lead us to condemn Utamaro and his fellows as immoral for producing such pictures, nor the public as lecherous because they purchased them: nor should we blind ourselves to the artistic worth of the *shunga*. It is true that at the period I am discussing there was something sophisticated and even perverted about the erotica that does not bear out the idea, as some would have it, of a primitive and blameless worship of the life-force, but in this field, as in so many others, the Ukiyo-e artist could not resist his weakness for burlesqueing and making game of the serious things of life.

The erotic picture-books of the Ukiyo-e artists can be traced back to early Tosa *makimono* in which twelve scenes, nominally one for each month, were enacted. Marriage scrolls or 'brides' books' are also older than the earliest Ukiyo-e *ehon*, which simply carried on a tradition, by wood-block printing, that had had its origin in the brush-drawn scrolls of the aristocracy. It may perhaps be maintained that these early paintings had an instructional intent, but in Edo times such a purpose was never expressed, except in parody.

Utamaro's reputation as a libertine has undoubtedly been based to a large extent upon his responsibility for a considerable number of albums of erotic pictures, but in fact it is doubtful if he designed a greater number than several other Ukiyo-e artists, certainly less, I would imagine,

from the numbers still extant, than Harunobu or Koryūsai.

Uta-makura ('*The Poem of the Pillow*'), published the same year as the *Insect Book*, 1788, was, like that album, most sumptuously produced and a miracle of colour-printing. It is, from every point of view, an astonishing collection of prints, in colour effects and style of drawing often utterly different from other works of the period, disturbing, revolting and yet fascinating at the same time.

No publisher is named, but it is fairly clear that it was Tsutajū; in fact he is unlikely to have allowed any other publisher to handle a work so outstanding when the artist was his own protégé and living under his roof. A double-page foreword begins the book, but the language it is couched in and the local and topical allusions conspire to make it unintelligible to us. But speaking of the title of the book, the writer says: 'I have gone far in order to bring the name of the painter near; *Uta-makura* and he shall be the servant of the awakening of spring.'[1]

Yet, if any other proof of authorship were lacking, the first print links it unmistakably with one of the most innocent and delightful signed triptychs of the period, that of *Girls watching awabi divers at Enoshima* (Fig. 31, page 47). In this first print, one of these charming fisher-girls, clad only in the red loin-cloth usual with them and her long black hair falling like a mantle over her shoulders, is seated on a rock beside her basket of *awabi* (shellfish). Although near enough inshore for a pine to overhang the rock with its decorative gnarled branches and green rosettes of needles, the water is abysmally deep, and the fisher-girl on the rock is watching a scene enacted beneath the waves that might well have caused her hair to rise in horror, but which actually appears to afford her slight amusement, politely hidden by her raised right hand. In the depths, another fisher-girl is being carried off by two ghouls called *Kappa*, too obviously human in certain respects, but with heads that are half-serpent, half-man, and feet and hands that are webbed and provided with talons. Kurth suggests that the scene is a dream of the fisher-girl on the bank, and mentions that these divers had a reputation for being very passionate. Certainly, above water all is idyllic, exquisite in form and colour, and below there is a distinctly nightmarish mingling of fair and foul.

[1] *Shunga* is translated literally as 'spring drawings'.

Another print, the raping of a girl by a gross, hairy man, is quite appalling in its effect. Set against a very dark, blue-grey background, the figures are stark, caught suddenly in a blaze of light against the empty night. De Goncourt thought the artist was personifying uxoriousness as a toad defiling a human being, and Kurth felt the vision belonged to the realm of fearsome dreams. It has an intensity and horror rare in Japanese art, and calls to mind some of the etchings of Goya.

Following this is a print (Pl. VI) that is, despite the compromising attitude of the couple, irresistibly charming—the colour, the dainty dresses, the diaphanous stuffs so perfectly rendered, make the print a delight, and there is little in it to offend anyone. The man in the picture has been identified with Utamaro himself though on no stronger grounds than the fact that the man's dress exactly resembles that which Utamaro is wearing in another print in which he is named (Fig. 77). It would, it is true, be in the taste of the period for the artist to portray himself *en galante posture* in this way, wafting a fan which bears a poem likening his plight to that of a crane whose beak has been gripped by a bivalve shell—'Its beak trapped by the shell, the bird cannot fly away.' But this identification with Utamaro is all surmise.

Perhaps the most offensive print is that of a strangely-garbed couple that are, obviously, and with malicious intent, meant to represent two Dutch lovers. Nagasaki had been opened to the Dutch nearly two hundred years earlier, but the foreigners, even in Utamaro's time, still seemed to have been regarded with a mixture of curiosity and contempt, amounting not infrequently to open animosity. Utamaro's Dutchman is a parody, not only of the fantastic dress of the intruder, but also of the European manner of drawing, there being a quite un-Japanese emphasis on 'likeness', an insistence on the detailed ugliness of the features, and even a sort of chiaroscuro to achieve those ends. The livid face with its bushy eyebrows, flamboyant moustache and powdered and curled wig, is surmounted by a black, red-bordered tricorne hat which completes a monstrous satire on the European as seen through Japanese eyes. And the woman is of ungainly form and repellent face, with none of the compensating grace that, in most of the prints, makes it easy for us to understand Utamaro's appeal to Edo youth.

One of the scenes has an outdoor background that might have come out of *Fugen-zō*, with all the cherry-trees in flower; two or three of the prints show the interior of typical Yoshiwara apartments, with evident signs of the evening's pleasure, the *sake*-service especially, littered about the rooms. Of these interiors, one is outstanding for its colour effect. A young man and his companion, both wearing dresses of exquisite hues, loom against a magnificent folding screen, decorated with flower and bamboo patterns, its bright yellow ground flooding the picture with sunshine.

I have dealt with *Uta-makura* in some detail as it is an exceptional work, showing yet more aspects of the vast talent and originality of these years. I shall not attempt to describe later *shunga*—the circumlocutory euphemisms begin to wear thin in any case, and no other book reaches quite the heights of *Uta-makura*, though the *Negai no Itoguchi* of 1799 comes close. Many of the *shunga* of Utamaro and other artists were cheap publications turned out for the masses, and the designing and colour-printing of these do nothing to make the contents acceptable in any way. Only the finer *shunga*, produced with the utmost care for the wealthy merchants and the samurai, are really worth consideration. Kiyoshi Shibui, the distinguished Japanese authority on Ukiyo-e, has devoted a lifetime to the study of the erotic books of the school, and the titles of Utamaro's books, together with reproductions, mostly expurgated, can be referred to in his *Ukiyoye Naishi* and two recent books on Utamaro. These, and other books that bear upon the subject, are listed in the Bibliography.

CHAPTER TEN

THE 'SHELL BOOK' AND
THE 'HUNDRED SCREAMERS'

ALTHOUGH in the West there is a long history of finely illustrated books, very few of these, since the introduction of printing, have been of what could be called the decorated kind, in which not only is each page consciously composed, the text married to the design to form a harmonious whole, but the pages themselves are linked by a unifying theme and system of decoration, giving a oneness to the whole production. The 'Kelmscott' Chaucer and some of the books decorated by Beardsley are of this kind, and in France a number of presses have, since the turn of the century, published the type of book that can be appreciated as an artistic whole, like any other work of art.

Examples of this kind of book are far commoner in Japan, as is to be expected of a people whose innate flair for pattern was expressed in the meanest articles of everyday use, and who were aided by the far greater freedom and decorative possibilities of their chirography compared with even the best of our type founts. In an artist's hands, their calligraphy lent itself to arabesque flourishes and impetuous bravura (often quite inimical to legibility). Although we can never be initiate where the art of chirography is concerned, a page of fine *hiragana* can be surprisingly impressive even to us.

Yet even among Japanese books, the *Shell Book* must be considered remarkable, hardly another has quite the same concinnity of subject, text and illustration, not even the *Insect Book* or the '*Hundred Screamers*'. Its title is a poetic one that strikes the chord for the whole work—*Shiohi no tsuto* ('*Gifts of the Ebb-tide*'). The poems were contributed by the members of a poetry club with whom it is pleasant to think that Utamaro was on familiar terms, if he was not actually a member himself.

In a foreword, Akera Kankō explains, in the exaggerated, high-flown language of this type of Japanese effusion, the genesis of this book of poems. As a literary curiosity, perhaps it will not be out of place to give a translation here:[1]

[1] By J. J. O'Brien Sexton in the *Burlington Magazine*, March 1918.

'There is a proverb which says that a field-mouse may become a Rice-bran bird or a Well-frog a ladle. In the beginning of spring several men assembled on the beach at Sode ga Ura in order to picnic and gather shells on the beach. Now who were these men? They were . . .' (here follow the names of several of the comic poem writers); 'in all we made a company of 36 who participated in the picnic. All these fellows were "low comedians" of the literary world—mere good-for-nothings. But when the wine-cups had circulated freely they all became gigantic birds (i.e. men of consequence, in their own estimation) and began to flap their wings which reached to the heavens. Accepting an invitation to the Dragon Palace under the sea we succeeded on our way to the bed of the ocean in gathering myriads of shells. We had such a jolly time during our 1000 years' sojourn there that it would be difficult matter indeed to tell to the folk at home all that happened. And so, to give vent to our happiness and at the same time to ease our wine-distended bellies, we have spouted out these songs about the shells that we have taken home as presents from the Bay of Shinagawa. Hence this volume.'

(signed) Akera Kankō

This is typical of the hyperbole and rodomontade with which the Japanese garnished their style, and rather unreliable material for assessing the kind of people who were Utamaro's companions at this time: it was almost part of the poet's stock in trade, his sanction for inspiration, that he looked freely on the wine when it was red. The effusive Akera says 'Hence this volume', but unfortunately, he is referring only to the poems, and we have no such interesting explanation of how Utamaro was given the task of immortalizing them.

After the foreword comes the first print, which is introductory to the main theme—the shells themselves. It is a picture of people gathering shells along Shinagawa bay at ebb-tide, and what more charming beach scene exists in art? The retreating sea, indicated by the most fragile washes of ultramarine,

37. Gathering shells along the shore of Shinagawa Bay. From the album *Gifts of the Ebb-Tide*. About 1790.

is ribbed with a perfectly apt blind-printing that casts minute shadows like shallow wavelets (Fig 37).

Then follow six pages that are designed to bring our eyes closer to the shells, as though on some propitious day the tide had been unusually prodigal and strewn the sand with a hoard of different treasures. The sea, receding to the top of each page in wine-coloured lines of conventional wave form lays bare the sand, sand powdered with gold-dust and glinting as if the water had indeed just washed over it. Stranded as if by the cast of the last wave are the 'gifts of the ebb-tide', shells of a wide variety of creatures, of fluted shellfish and whorled snail, *awabi*, mussels, scallops, 'cherry-blossoms' and other shells of quaint shape and translucent colour known to us by unpoetic Latin names (Figs. 38, 39).

Every device of the printer's art and artifice is used to embellish the shells. Gold and mica dusts overlay faint tinges of rose that shine through with a suffused glow, the nacre of the *awabi* has an iridescent lustre, tiny garlands of button-like shells glimmer and sparkle with a wet sheen, others have the fragility of a dragonfly's wing, with fretted shining surface; furrowed or encrusted, silvered or gold-dusted, the shells almost trespass into the

realm of the lacquerer's art, with its subtleties of variegated texture and inlay work.

Across the wavy lines of the retreating sea (lines, by the way, omitted from the second edition) a poem is written on each of the prints, centred on one of the shells depicted. Were the poems inspired by the drawings, did the company of 'dissolute' poets have the good fortune—denied us—of seeing Utamaro's own drawings before the engravings were made?

As the first plate was the induction to the pages of treasure-trove, so the last is a sort of epilogue. The party has returned from the beach and the girls sit in a circle around shells arranged in concentric rings upon the floor, representing a certain stage in the popular shell-game called *kai-awase*.

J. J. O'Brien Sexton, whose word on such matters is to be respected, wrote of this book: 'From a technical point of view, it is in my opinion, the finest example of wood-engraving and colour-printing that the world has ever seen.'

The two plates with figures are of interest, too, as probably marking the last appearance in Utamaro's work of the type of girl of tiny, unexaggerated form that belongs to the first half of his

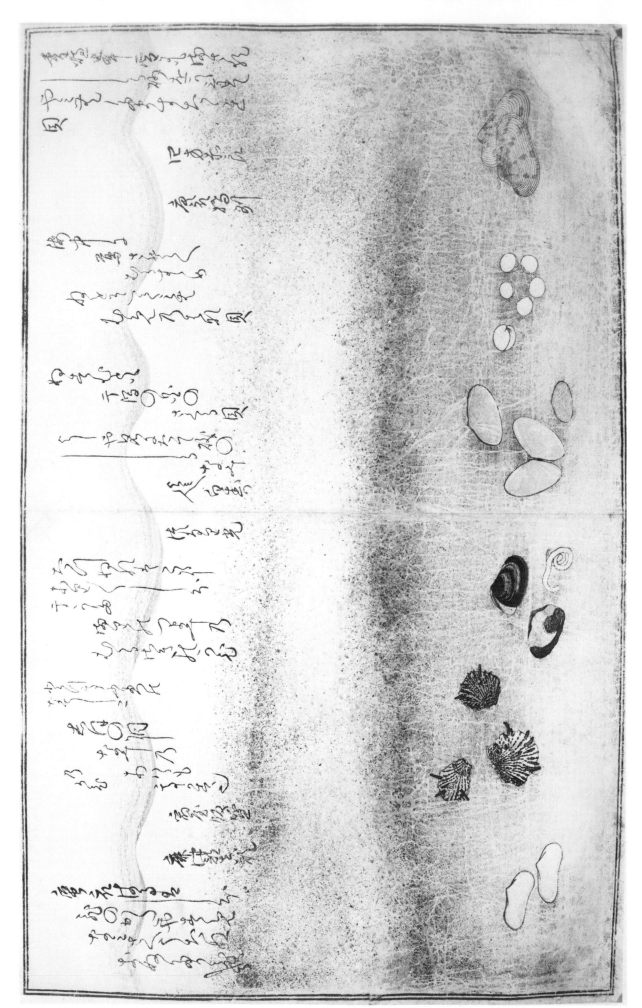

38. Sea-shells. From the album Gifts of the Ebb-Tide. About 1790.

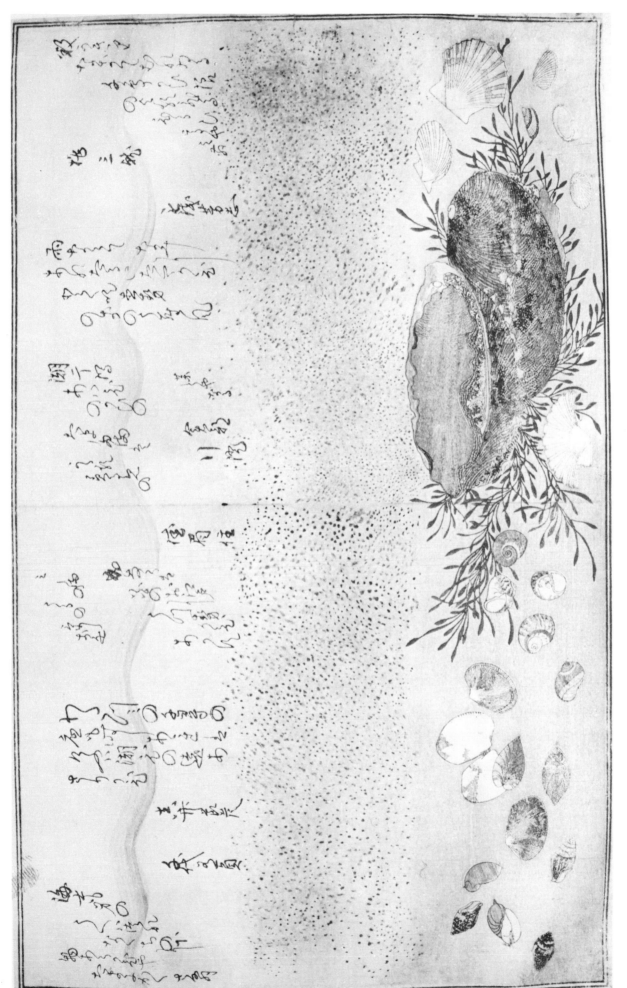

35. *Shells and sea-weed.* From the album *Gifts of the Ebb-Tide.* About 1790.

40. *Japan wren and two snipe. From the album* Birds Compared in Humorous Ditties. *About* 1791.

career, and above all, to the albums. Some doubt exists as to the date of *Shiohi no tsuto*, but the style of hairdressing points to 1790 (compare the fashions of the shell-gatherers on Shinagawa beach with those in a dated book of this year, *Fugen-zō* or *Ehon Azuma Asobi* and the similarity is apparent) and the dog may have been introduced into the last plate to indicate the Dog-year, which fell in 1790. By the time of the half-length portraits discussed in the next chapter, Utamaro had forsaken the amiable little girls of the eighties, and with them depart almost the last traces of the Kiyonaga influence. Henceforth, the woman to whom Utamaro devotes his art almost exclusively is more sophisticated and worldly, more elegant and imposing, and often disturbing in a way that the little charmers of the albums were not.

The *Momo chidori kyōka awase* ('One Hundred Birds compared in Humorous Ditties', more commonly known as '*The Hundred Screamers*') completes Utamaro's trilogy of 'nature' albums. Although, like the *Shell Book*, undated, there are good reasons for assuming that it appeared in 1791. Two volumes comprise the work, and at the back of each the publisher, Tsutajū, inserted a page of advertisements of other choice books bearing his imprint. Among the books advertised are Utamaro's *Ehon Gin-Sekai* (published, as mentioned in Chapter VII, in the spring of 1790) and also Shigemasa's *Ehon Fukujusō*, published in the early months of 1791.

Although, with the *Shell Book* in our hands, we are ready to accept it as the *ultima Thule* of the colour wood-block printer's art, when we turn the soft, far too damageable pages of the *Bird Book*, we are bound to allow that they must share in that high assessment. The *Bird Book* is not, as are the *Insect* and *Shell* books, without comparable precedent; one book with at least apparently similar material preceded Utamaro's, and rivals this in the beauty of the designs and the superlative colour-printing—Kitao Masayoshi's *Ehon Kachō Kagami* ('A Picture-Book mirroring Flowers and Birds')—first published in 1789. For a long time, in fact, the plates of Masayoshi's *Ehon*, unsigned and invariably found detached from the excessively rare first edition (where the authorship is placed beyond doubt), were ascribed to Utamaro, though a comparison of the two books shows a quite decisive difference in draughtsmanship.

Masayoshi, a pupil of Shigemasa, copied his birds from certain paintings by Kiyō Ishōsai Shūsen, but the colour wood-engravings are probably the only other Ukiyo-e works in this genre that can hold their own in company with Utamaro's. Whether Utamaro received any inspiration from Masayoshi's book will probably never be decided, though that he knew it I do not doubt. But however interesting a comparison of Masayoshi's and Utamaro's respective treatment of a common theme, it is rather outside the scope of this book. Another interesting topic, their position in relation to the bird-and-flower prints in the *ehon* of such classical artists as Kanyōsai and Suiseki, can only be touched on. The enthusiasts for the books of the classical artists, artists who sought their inspiration in the works of the Chinese masters, often show a tendency to belittle the Ukiyo-e for no better reason, as far as can be judged, than that the Ukiyo-e style differs from the Chinese. Thus, in a lecture to the Japan Society[1] Mr Holloway, comparing Utamaro's birds to Kanyōsai's, said 'His birds make Utamaro's look like the Yoshiwara creatures they are by comparison', which is nothing to the point, because a 'Yoshiwara creature' from the hand of Utamaro can be a greater work of art than a dull Chinese princess from a classicist's. The style is different, but each style has its own excellencies: there is little gained by 'placing' these schools in a table of absolute aesthetic values: individuals in any case override such easy theories.

Utamaro's birds are real, not abstract birds: there has been no sacrifice of truth, the most delicate shades of colour and the softest down of feather are rendered with wonderful accuracy: yet as in the *Insect Book*, each double page is composed so that birds, plants, and the *hiragana* of the verses form one perfect pattern (Fig. 40; Pl. VII).

[1] Printed in the *Bulletin of the Japan Society*, June 1955.

CHAPTER ELEVEN

THE HALF-LENGTH 'PORTRAITS'
1791–1793

SOON AFTER 1790, Utamaro designed some series of half-length 'portraits' that in certain ways marked a greater departure from tradition than any of his works before or after, and include prints that have always been considered among the most delightful and individual of any from his hand.

With rare exceptions, no means exist of dating prints with the certainty that books can be dated, and we are under the necessity of relying on 'internal evidence'. With Utamaro, this consists of fashions in hairstyles, changes in signature and occurrence of censor seals, on all of which a measure of agreement can be expected; and depends also on changes in the style and expressiveness of his drawing, in respect of which intangible qualities it is natural that divergent views should be held.

The Ukiyo-e artist, fortunately for us, almost invariably signed his prints—the panel of decorative characters is a concomitant in the design—and after his name, it was customary to add one of three characters, *ga*, *hitsu*, or *zu*, meaning 'drawn', 'painted with the brush' or 'illustration', just as our artists or engravers add '*pinxit*' or '*sculpsit*' to their signatures. Utamaro rarely used the third of these signs. It is not easy for us to tell exactly what shade of difference the *ga* and *hitsu* held for the Japanese, for, in relation to the print designs, the characters stood apparently for the same thing; but certainly *hitsu* was more the painter's prerogative than the print-designer's, and perhaps its use by Utamaro was an expression of his growing self-importance. All Utamaro's earlier works are signed with the *ga* sign, but about 1791–2 he switched to *hitsu* and only rarely reverted to the other.

A perceptible difference can be detected between the early and the late signatures of most Japanese artists. With Utamaro, there is a gradual change which seems to express the development of the artist, and if one could trust those who deduce character from handwriting, materials exist covering the whole of his life from early manhood to death. Apart from the 'Toyoaki' signatures of his first essays, he usually signed *Uta-maro*, generally in two characters, occasionally in three, breaking the *maro* into two. The illustrations show the variations in his calligraphy from the neat, square characters of the earliest signature, through the growing boldness and assurance of the first prints with *hitsu*, to the swagger and slovenliness of the last. There is, of course, no possibility of dating prints with precision from the signature alone, but it is a guide by which they can be roughly segregated into periods, especially useful with works that cannot be dated by the usual 'internal evidence': for instance, prints of animals, birds and flowers, and prints (like that of the *Three Chinese Heroes* reproduced as Fig. 14) in the Kanō style.

The censorship of prints, in common with all printed matter, had been in force for many years before Utamaro's day, but late in 1790, following a tightening up of the regulations, it became law that prints were to be stamped with the censor's seal, the small circular seal bearing the character *kiwame* (approved). It follows that prints bearing this seal belong to 1790 or later, but unfortunately its absence is not an altogether reliable proof that a print is anterior to 1790 in date, since many known to be later are without it, presumably because the censor had been evaded (often the case with 'pirated' prints).

The first of the series of half-length portraits of tea-house beauties and courtesans have the *ga* addition to the signature, and are stamped with the *kiwame* seal: both confirmatory of the attributions to the year 1791–2, which in any case the hair-dressing fashions and the style of drawing point to.

It smacks of pedantry to insist on such chronological details, but in putting forward these prints as representing a distinct innovation it is obviously necessary to establish their date.

Though not, perhaps, the very earliest of this type, two early series are of outstanding beauty, and have always stood high in the estimation of connoisseurs: those entitled *Fujin sō gaku jittai* ('*Ten Learned Studies of Women*') and *Fujin ninsō jippin* ('*Ten Types of Women's Physiognomies*'). There is a triple novelty

婦人相學十躰
浮気之相
相見
歌麿画

41. *The Passionate Type*. From the series *Ten Learned Studies of Women*. About 1792–3.

in Utamaro's presentation of women in these plates—the half-length figure was itself almost unknown; the mica background, if not absolutely Utamaro's invention, had only been used very occasionally by other masters before; and finally, these prints purported to be portraits, if not of individuals, then of moods, or of character.

Portraiture, a 'likeness' in the Western manner, was hardly ever attempted by Japanese artists: there were rare exceptions, such as the occasional portraits of a priest or a memorial portrait of some personage of note, posthumously painted and probably quite unreliable, and even these instances, owing to the technique of the East, would be far from satisfying our conceptions of portraiture. It is, in fact, just another manifestation of the fundamental differences between the Eastern and Western approaches to painting: in keeping with their eternal compromise between naturalism and conventionalized form in order to achieve balance and pattern in their compositions. Faces detailed in feature and expression would conflict with this paramount requirement; they took their place like hands and arms; they had to be without undue emphasis. Perhaps this inevitable sacrifice of portraiture is a limitation to regret in Japanese art, but it was a sacrifice made quite naturally by them in their singleness of aim. We must not expect the heart-searching drawing, the fidelity to character, of say Rembrandt or Velázquez, but in its place we are given arrangements of the human figure in terms of line and colour such as even the greatest Europeans rarely achieved.

Not that it is true, of course, that the faces are all alike. Each artist developed his own particular style of drawing the human head, selected his ideal and, within the self-imposed limits, evoked a certain mild expressiveness. The canons of etiquette in Japan, leading to the impassivity of countenance, may be partly responsible; perhaps, owing to the relative purity of the race (compared, for example, with our own) and the general conformity to a norm, there was only a very narrow range within which variety in facial features could be denoted: but the expressionlessness and lack of variety in feature is due more to the style of drawing by outline.

However, it is one of the delights of a study of Japanese prints to be able to recognize each artist's work by the particular ideal to which he gave preference. Since Moronobu, each great artist had contributed a new figure to the Ukiyo-e gallery of idealized womanhood (and in this the head was but one, if to us the most telling, part); a personage as unmistakably his own as his signature. To create a type was almost a mark of greatness. Moronobu perhaps set the style for the whole school of followers: a woman of elegance in which face and hands and flowing flowered robe was, like a figure in a dance, appreciated more for its grace of movement than for any especial beauty of feature. The Kaigetsūdo group invested their courtesans with the statuesque immobility of Grecian goddesses whose slightest gesture is significant and whose pose varies but slightly in the small but wonderful series of prints they made. On the other hand, Sukenobu, his near contemporary, filled book after book with a multitude of charming, sweet-faced girls, familiar friendly creatures, warm-hearted, out to please; and Morrison says of them: 'The great family likeness in most of the kindly, innocent faces of his girls has been pointed out as a fault, but I see no fault in it. It was the way of the Ukiyo-e artists to seek each his own type of female beauty and to maintain it as his ideal. For this reason the amateur with very small experience may readily separate the works of the leading painters and though at first European eyes may see little in these faces but a sameness and lack of expression, a reasonable acquaintance and sympathetic study will reveal the infinite subtle variety and the quiet meaning that inform the seemingly quaint and stolid features.'

And so with all the masters who devoted themselves to the depiction of Japanese women, Okamura Masanobu, Shigenaga, Harunobu, Koryūsai, Kiyonaga, Utamaro, Eishi, we find this sort of 'family likeness' running through the countless damsels of each artist's prints, and one should not ask for more; it is one of the conventions of their art, like the flat washes of colour, the expressive line.

Until this time, 1791–2, Utamaro's ideal was one that had recognizable affinities with those of a number of earlier masters, but principally Kiyonaga. It is still possible to single out his early prints, even unsigned, from those whose influence he most felt, but the distinctiveness is more in compositional effects than in the manner of drawing the women. But with the two series we are considering, Utamaro created an unmistakably original type, whose expressiveness, compared with those of his forerunners,

VII. *A domestic cock and hen, and Japan bunting [Hōjiro] on a bamboo stake. From the book Birds Compared in Humorous Ditties. About* 1791.

VIII. *The tea-house waitress O-hisa.* 1791–2.

婦女人相十品

相觀 歌麿考画

42. *Beauty smoking.* From the series *Ten Types of Women's Physiognomies.* 1792–3.

43. *Newly-married girl admiring her lacquered teeth in a mirror.*
From the series *Ten Learned Studies of Women*. About 1792–3.

justified the high-sounding titles they bear; and that Utamaro was conscious of the difference between these figures and all that the Ukiyo-e school had produced so far, the manner in which they are signed bears witness. 'Thoughtfully drawn by Utamaro, the Physiognomist' are the words he uses on one set, and on the other the imprint has a similar sense.

Let it at once be admitted that, however much we may, in the light of the titles, be tempted to read character into these winsome faces (and some have allowed their desire to eulogize Utamaro to

44. O-kita, a teahouse girl. 1792–3.

run away with their imaginations) they are still, by our standards, very far from being 'portraits', the manner of drawing is still unquestionably Japanese, with the invariable three-quarter face view, the simple outline of brow and cheek, narrow eyes, single line to give the nose, and half-parted petal-like lips: hierarchic, drawn to a formula: and yet they are just as unquestionably Utamaro's addition to the Ukiyo-e gallery of beauties, and have a range of *expression* far wider and more intense than any Ukiyo-e artist's hitherto.

Much has been made by collectors of the silver

mica-ground of these two and other series to be mentioned later. As I have said, mica had been used earlier, as the background of at least one print of Okumura Masonobu's half a century earlier, and as touches in books relatively common in the preceding two decades, but if not Utamaro's invention, he was the first to use it with anything like regularity. It was not until 1794 that Sharaku, Chōki and Shunchō began to use the mica background.

The object was probably to claim by one further device the attention of the novelty-loving Edo folk, and in their original state (and so few remain anywhere near that) the bright metallic surface must have been attractive in itself, giving a hint of preciousness, of extravagance; but to Utamaro, probably the most important effect was the way the silver background, burnished almost like a mirror, shone in the light, so that the figure came forward in bold relief, like a figure against a sun-bright sky— an effect not without reaction on the colours of the dresses, which are subdued and given unimaginable nuances as they loom against the silver.

Sadly, very few of the prints remaining are in anything approaching their original condition. The silver-ground tarnishes or flakes off, and does not mellow as the colours do with age, and the result, in inferior prints, is distressing.

The best known of these two series have been reproduced many times, but I make no excuse for including some again. That in Fig. 41 is from the *Fujin sō gaku jittai*, from a wonderfully preserved copy in the British Museum. How unerringly this figure is placed upon the page, how masterly the drawing (note especially the rendering of the piled-up black hair and the solidity it gives, without recourse to shadows, to the head). In another from this set, a girl in a red-and-white checked dress and magnificent green sash patterned with gold swastikas, is blowing a 'poppen', a tiny trumpet that made two sounds, 'pop' and 'pen'. Her long sleeve swings out as she raises the poppen to her lips and helps to build the monumental pyramid that Utamaro used as a basis for a number of his most consummate designs.

Another famous print from this series is a girl holding a mirror in her right hand and admiring the reflection of her blackened teeth which she clenches as she opens her lips (Fig. 43). There is a singular intentness in her gaze, reminiscent of another superb print of a year or two later of two women, back to back, dressing their hair before mirrors with an absorption in their task that is rendered with extraordinary power (Fig. 46).

From the other series, I will mention two. For me, the finest print of either set is the portrait of the girl with a long tobacco-pipe in her right hand (Fig. 42). She too is negligently dressed, the loose green-blue garment, decorated with the starfish pattern, is open to her waist, where it is held by a carelessly knotted red girdle. Her hair is in a state of 'undress' with a curious knot at the front, and she makes a slight *moue* as she puffs the smoke from the corner of her mouth (smoke which is so delicately printed that few impressions retain any sign of it). The easy pose, the right forearm held upright, with the long pipe falling at an angle between the fingers, the left hand dreamily rearranging the folds of the wrap across her shoulders, is expressive of the lassitude of a mid-day rising after a night of pleasure, and the languor of this young but experienced face is wonderfully interpreted.

Another is of a married woman (denoted by her shaved eyebrows) holding a letter high in front of her eyes as she reads it. She has a blue dress stippled with white dots, and an undergarment of purple shows at the neck. Her sash is yellow and patterned with a conventional design in black. Even the dress patterns are noticeably different in these series, the sprinkled petals, dots, checks and shell motifs, if not new, are all applied in an original way.

But the chief merit of these prints in our eyes is something that springs only indirectly from the use of the three-quarter length figure, the mica ground and the exquisite patterns of the dresses: we marvel most at the placing of these single figures against a plain background in such a way as to create effective and sometimes monumental designs, a feat that has perhaps lost some of its surprise owing to our familiarity with modern examples of the same order in, for instance, the lithographs of Toulouse-Lautrec, the posters of the Beggarstaff Brothers, and the paintings of Degas and other Impressionists.

The girl admiring her teeth in the mirror (Fig. 43) still stirs us with its daring, but how startling in its originality must it have been to the Edo public when it first made its appearance. It is this wonderful ability to compose telling and even moving designs with the simple elements provided by single figures, or by two or three together, that is probably Utamaro's greatest gift, a power that lifts these early mica series, and even more, the astonish-

當時三美人

富本豊ひな
難波屋きた
高しまひさ

45. *Three Beauties of the Present Day:*
Tomimoto Toyohina, Takashima Ohisa and Naniwaya Okita. 1792–3.

46. *Two Girls dressing their hair before mirrors*. About 1793.

ing sets of a few years later of pairs of famous lovers,[1] into a realm of their own in Japanese art.

The girls of these early sets are anonymous, but we have ample evidence of whom Utamaro had in mind when he made the designs. The tea-house attendants O-kita, O-chie and O-hisa were the friends as well as the models of the artist and appear time after time in the prints of the period, and singers like Toyohina rivalled the tea-house girls in his affections. It is these, rather than the courtesans, who form the subjects of the mica-ground prints.

In other mica-background prints of roughly the same date as the *Ten Types of Women's Physio-gnomies* the three tea-house girls mentioned are named, and no doubt they were as popular among the Edo men-of-the-world as the courtesans. In a print with the title *Three Beauties of the Day* (Fig. 45), Utamaro has arranged the heads of O-hisa, O-kita and Toyohina in a pyramid, a device that he had already used most effectively in a slightly earlier series, also on a mica ground, of geisha per-forming their burlesque 'Niwaka' festival, in which, however, the figures are half-length. Another gives the portraits of seven geisha girls.

O-hisa and O-kita too, are the girls that appear in two double-sided prints (*ryōmenzuri*) with the front view of the girl printed on one side and a back view on the reverse, exactly corresponding in line with the other. One of these little *jeux d'esprit*, as charming as they are eccentric, shows O-hisa dressed in a black gown with the white criss-cross markings in vogue at this period, with a green over-skirt like an apron, and white flower pattern that spreads from the hem upwards. Her sash is tied behind the body, as befits an 'honest' woman. This print is among the rarest of Utamaro's, but a good facsimile can be referred to in Kurth's book. In the print of O-kita she is shown in her everyday role as a waitress at the *cha-ya* (tea-house), bearing a cup of tea upon a tray.

But the loveliest depictions of Utamaro's favour-ites are, to my mind, those that appeared a little

[1] See Chapter XV.

later—perhaps the very first prints to be signed Utamaro *hitsu*. These again are half-length portraits on a mica ground but bear poems in long narrow panels to one side of the print.

O-kita is again shown bearing a tea-cup upon a tray, supported this time by both hands held before her (Fig. 44). He must be cold indeed who is not touched by the winsome figure so gracefully advanc-ing to serve her guests. Her hair is dressed in the elaborate but attractive style of the day—it is a masterpiece of artifice and betokens hours before the mirror. Her blue mantle is sprinkled with white paulinia flowers, her black-figured sash spreads behind her like a train. She is the personification of all those exquisite creatures who devoted their days and nights to ministering to the bloods of Edo, or in preparing their persons to do so. And O-hisa, in a companion print no less attractive, smiles in-genuously over her fan, robed in apparel that Uta-maro contrives to make quite regal in its splendid colour and solemnity of line (Pl. VIII).

Another of the half-length portraits of this series is a portrait of the courtesan Hana-ōgi ('Flower-fan') of Ōgi-ya, depicted by nearly every great Ukiyo-e artist from Koryūsai's time some ten or fifteen years earlier, and by Utamaro's day almost a legendary figure. She is shown holding the narrow strip of paper called *tanzaku* on which poems were inscribed, and lowers the long writing brush with an abstracted air as if searching for inspiration. Her apparel is rich and touched here and there with shining mica, which sets off the deep violet of her dress and the yellow *obi* decorated with hō-ō birds in black. Her hair is dressed in an unusual 'helmet' style, and much bedizened with long stiletto-like pins. In the top right-hand corner there are two cartouches, one giving the courtesan's name and 'house', the other a poem, the drift of which (with erotic suggestiveness, as ever) is as follows:

When Autumn entered my heart,
Then I wandered into obscure paths
And look! as the night engulfed me
Hana-ōgi came into flower!

CHAPTER TWELVE

THE GLORIFICATION OF WOMAN
1793–1795

IN THE FOLLOWING YEARS, Utamaro's art was devoted almost exclusively to the glorification of woman, and an immense number of single prints, and of series of prints, form a gallery of beauties drawn mainly from the pleasure quarters, but including also ordinary housewives and their daughters who, like those in the *Girls preparing stuffs for dresses*, provide some of his most alluring models.

However great as a designer, Utamaro owed his outstanding popularity with the Edo public to the fact that he created a woman more infatuating than those of his predecessors and contemporaries. As I have suggested earlier, we are in no position to judge the physical appeal of this woman to those who came under her spell. Although to them she seems to have been the essence of femininity, to us she appeals more because of her exquisite trappings, the patterned dresses, the brocaded sashes, the fantastic coiffures, and the elegant movement and studied gesture by which such adornments were displayed. The woman created by Constantin Guys, drawn as often as not, like Utamaro's, from the *demi-monde*, has a certain relationship with Utamaro's in other respects, and it is not perhaps surprising that Baudelaire's words, *à propos* of this artist, can be applied equally well to Utamaro: 'Everything used by woman for her adornment becomes part of herself; the artists who have applied themselves to the study of this enigmatic being have been as much under the spell of everything in the feminine universe, as ever they were under that of woman herself.' The events and emotions portrayed in Japanese prints are rarely of a deeply moving kind, in fact, we, in our ignorance of Japanese literature and custom, may often miss the subtler allusions; and in this welding into one of woman and 'everything used by her for her adornment', the single figures, certainly, often tend to lose their identity as human beings and have significance only as elements in an abstract design; whilst, in the compositions involving two or more figures, the linkage between the figures, the flow of action and sometimes the evident flow of thought, can create the illusion of abstractions possessing a life of their own, and inhabiting a world where all is unreal and strange to us.

But Utamaro has that power, rare among Japanese artists, of breaking through the abstraction, of bringing us into intimacy with his sitters, of giving the illusion of life as *we* know it, so that under the brocade we can sense the breathing woman. This is one of Utamaro's distinguishing marks in the field of *bijin-ga* (Pictures of Beautiful Women). Koechlin, who showed if anything a preference for Kiyonaga in a comparison with Utamaro, put his finger upon this when he wrote: 'That which the beauties of Kiyonaga's Yoshiwara are doing hardly interests us, they deign to be so little amused by it. Those of Utamaro are all action, the affair of the moment, however slight it may be, which absorbs all their attention, holds ours too, and though they are less noble and less magnificent, and though the art is singularly less classic, they "speak" to us more.'

As an example, one might cite a lovely print from the series *Seirō Setsu Gekka* ('*Snow, Moon and Flowers of the Green Houses*'), under which fanciful title the artist portrays beauties of the Yoshiwara as the personifications of the beauties of nature. Kasugano of Tama House, in a deep black kimono decorated towards the hem with a chrysanthemum pattern, kneels at her writing table, brush poised in hand, looking at the fan she has just decorated with a poem. Her hair is dressed in the 'butterfly' style, then just making its appearance among ladies of fashion. At her side stands Uraba, her *shinzō*, tall and slim, an exceptionally charming figure, one hand clasped above the other as she slightly inclines her head to read what Kasugano has written on the fan. There is a tenseness in this figure, as though the girl has caught her breath at her mistress's audacity: these two are living creatures, and there is a flow of unspoken thought between them (Fig. 47).

Whatever the differing causes of their popularity with the Edokko of the East and us in the West, these prints of *bijin-ga*, when issued, were immensely

青楼雪月花

玉屋内

春日野

うらゝ
初ゝ

歌麿筆

47. *The beauty Kasugano inscribing a fan.*
From the scries *Snow, Moon and Flowers of the Green Houses*. 1793–5.

48. *Two girls dancing at the New Year.*
(The left-hand figure is by Shunchō, the right-hand
by Utamaro.) 1791–2.

subjects treated, among which certain triptychs of the Genji Romance, *à la mode*, are notable. Whether, as has been stated, he led the fashion for 'extreme tallness and slenderness', or whether he borrowed the mannerism from Kiyonaga or Utamaro, he was undoubtedly one of the leaders of Ukiyo-e and a force to reckon with until about 1800. At that time, he forsook print-designing for brush-painting, for which he had a special flair, and produced some of the finest paintings of the whole Ukiyo-e school.

In some of the yellow-ground prints, too, there is a reminiscence of Kiyonaga, possibly the result of an admiration for one of Kiyonaga's aptest pupils, Shunchō, originally a follower of Shunshō, from whom he derived his name. As of so many of these contemporaries of Utamaro whose work has become famous, almost nothing is known of Shunchō, not even the dates of his birth and death; but that

49. *The waitress O-hisa and tea-house guests.* 1790–1.

successful. Hereafter there are so many that it would be impossible to mention them all. Instead, some of the most characteristic will be singled out.

About the time of the silver-ground portraits, Utamaro began also to employ a yellow ground. This may have been suggested by the prints of another contemporary, Chōbunsai Eishi, from an association with whom Utamaro may have gained more than has been generally conceded, though Eishi equally benefited from a sort of 'exchange of gifts'. With Eishi, this especial gift was an aristocratic refinement coupled with a powerful sinuous line that betrayed his early training in the Kanō school. A few years older than Utamaro, he came of samurai stock and his work, after an early surrender to the all-powerful Kiyonaga influence, showed the mark of breeding not only in the elegance of pose, line and colour, but even in the

50. *The courtesan Hana-murasaki ('Violet flower')*. One of a set of *Six Jewel-Rivers*. 1793–4.

he was on friendly terms with Utamaro soon after 1790 is proved by the existence of a print of *Two girls dancing at the New Year* designed jointly, one figure being drawn by Utamaro, the other by Shunchō. It is tempting to discover in this print the characteristics we expect from Utamaro and from a close follower of Kiyonaga; at any rate, the more mobile dancing figure of the two was given to Utamaro; but in facial detail there is little noticeable difference (Fig. 48).

The print where this facial type persists depicts Utamaro's favourite, O-hisa of Takashima House and her two guests (Fig. 49). She is standing before them with both hands raised to cover a smile, her figure tall and willowy and reminding one of Geffroy's phrase 'the curve of a sabre' in describing the pose, that slight sway from the hips and backward inclination of the upper part of the body that suggests mobility even in a standing figure. One of her attendants is proffering tea to her on a tray held out with both hands, another is seated upon a bench holding a yellow fan. A feature of this print, and a companion (like the other, in the British Museum), is the wonderful delicacy of printing shown in the white floral pattern picked out on the green, violet and blue dresses.

The resemblance to Shunchō is perhaps superficial only and no more than a passing phase, and soon this rather mild and even insipid face disappears from Utamaro's prints.

Under the title of *Mu Tamagawa* ('*Six Jewel-rivers*') Utamaro designed a set early in the decade which reaches a high-water mark of colour-printing. The '*Six Jewel-rivers*' is a title which exemplifies a curious habit of the Ukiyo-e artists who often seem to have been at pains first to make the title as recondite as possible—as in this case, where the six Tama rivers in various provinces of Japan (the 'Jewel-rivers', each traditionally associated with a bird, a flower, a custom, a poem) are portrayed by six famous courtesans; and then, to make the connection between title and picture as slender as possible, leaving it to the skill of the beholder to discover the link. In one print, for example, the pattern on the girl's robe is the clue.

Perhaps the loveliest of the series is that of Hana Murasaki. The courtesan is kneeling in what might almost be called the 'Eishi' pose, one leg folded under, the other raised but bent double at the knee, the long curved line of angled thigh given with a

51. *Girls preparing stuff for dresses*. Triptych. About 1794–6.

single splendid sweep of the brush (Fig. 50). The courtesan's name, 'Violet Flower', is given in a cartouche, and in the circle is the poem: 'Ah me, the lover that promises to come again tomorrow, he is like a wave gliding on the Tama stream'.

In these, and in the remaining prints of the series, there are just two figures, the courtesan and her companion, and Utamaro's resource in grouping them against the sulphur-yellow background is astonishing. Here, indeed, Utamaro portrays an ideal of tall, elegant womanhood that cannot be faulted on the score of exaggeration or distortion, and had he remained faithful to her, as Shunchō remained faithful all his career to *his* engaging mild-face type, Utamaro would have had fewer detractors—and we should have lost untold masterpieces. But it was not in Utamaro's nature to stand

still nor to remain faithful to one type, however beautiful. In another rare series a year or two later we see him flirting with a figure more attenuated and sinuous than before, and a flowing line that verges on mannerism. This is another set of six entitled *Natori Sake Rok'kasen*, a title that has puzzled most scholars. It has been translated: '*Name adoption of the Six Sake-house Poetesses*', the inference being that the prints were to celebrate the adoption of new names by the courtesans represented, but it is doubtful if the rather cryptic words are capable of any more definite meaning than a coupling of the well-known courtesans with favourite brands of *sake*, possibly with the idea of advertisement. At the top of each print is a small barrel of *sake* in its straw case, bearing the maker's name in large black characters, with a flowering branch of a tree on one side and to the right a red lacquer *sake* cup, seen in perspective, upon which is the name of the series. A double tablet gives the name of the particular *sake* and that of the courtesan. Here the thread between title and subject is so tenuous as to escape us (Pl. IX).

On each print is the figure of a seated or kneeling girl in a pose, as de Goncourt pointed out, resembling that of 'supporters' in our heraldic achievements. In certain of the prints, Utamaro has deliberately unbalanced the composition by placing the figure to one side against the straight bounding line of the print, a common enough practice now, familiar to us from Beardsley's and a host of subsequent variations on the device, but quite disturbing earlier, even to so enlightened an observer as Koechlin, who thought that in this series 'the search for elegance borders on mannerism'. But the mannerism is perhaps more noticeable in the flowing expressive line, in which the artist seems to have intended to out-Eishi Eishi, and succeeded in making the figures curiously disembodied, etherealized. But if we are right in attributing this series to the early nineties, the attenuation seems to have been an isolated experiment, or at least not to have been developed systematically as it was a few years later when the *Twelve Hours of the Yoshiwara* and kindred prints were designed.

A feature of this set is the unusually extensive employment of deep gauffrage to indicate the patterns of the garments. Gauffrage suffers more in the passage of time than the colours, for whereas the colours lose their pristine depth of hue only to take on new harmonies as the violets and blues fade to quiet buffs and greys, the pressure of the years robs many of the keen edge of the blind-printing, and delicate patterns are lost altogether or can only just be seen when the light falls on them from a certain angle.

About 1794 appeared one of Utamaro's loveliest works, the triptych of *Women preparing stuffs for dresses* of which there is an exceptionally well-preserved specimen in the British Museum (Fig. 51).

The triptych had become, by Utamaro's time, one of the favourite forms of Ukiyo-e art and adorned many a screen and sliding panel in the flimsy Japanese houses of the artisan and middle classes. The classic painters of the past had been in the habit of designing three *kakemono* with a connecting theme, each painting usually being designed independently. The Ukiyo-e artists went further and contrived to run their design across the three sheets, whilst at the same time, by their innate sense of pattern, managing to render each single sheet satisfying in itself, losing little or nothing by the detachment from the whole. Some single sheets, in fact, have existed as independent works without a suspicion that they originally formed part of a three-sheet design until another sheet has come to light unexpectedly that joins with it, or by title or other mark indicates that the whole was composed of three sheets.

Each sheet of *Women preparing stuffs for dresses* is singularly happy in arrangement, but when the triptych is seen as a whole the effectiveness of the composition is most impressive. The two figures in the centre, especially the girl in a grey

dress, are balanced by the two pyramidal groups on either side, in each case composed of a tall girl with a child playing at her feet (one can even find the counterpart of the circular mirror on one side in the fan on the other); note too how the centre sheet is linked to the right-hand section by the length of bright cloth held between the two girls' hands, and to the left-hand by the way in which the girl holding the insect cage turns towards the slightly isolated figure to attract her attention and, incidentally, to 'bring her into the picture'. The long trailing piece of gauze this latter girl is examining spreads into the centre sheet to make yet a further bond.

But the mastery of composition apart, how few of Utamaro's contemporaries could have attempted a scene of such intimate domesticity, could have captured that intentness upon their task which absorbs these girls, or have counterbalanced their seriousness so aptly with the delightful by-play of the children? In this particular vein, Utamaro was the natural inheritor of Harunobu's mantle, and, indeed, he was the last of the Ukiyo-e line worthily to wear it.

Another domestic scene is given in the diptych known as *The Kitchen*, probably a little later in date than the triptych just described. In this diptych there is a liveliness and bustle rare even for Utamaro.

In connection with Utamaro's indebtedness to Harunobu, there is an interesting print of two young *komusō*, each carrying in one hand a huge straw hat. To the right is written 'Designed by Harunobu' and to the left 'copied by Utamaro', but the tall elongated figures with their coiffures of the latest style are such as Harunobu never depicted or even dreamed of and one wonders what strange whim prompted Utamaro to make this palpable adaptation. Probably it was simply intended as 'homage to Harunobu', and in the manner of Ukiyo-e, took the form of 'Harunobu à la mode'.

During the period 1791 to 1793 we are without the guide to dating prints provided by printed books, but in 1794 there is one print in a book of *kyōka*, *Haru-no Iro* ('*The Colour of Spring*') and one print that can reasonably be dated 1795 or shortly after. This is a print (one sheet of a five-sheet print) of women visiting the temple at Asakusa and stopping before the statue of Fujin, the 'God of Wind', which, with the God of Thunder, Raijin, guards the portals. On one of the pillars is the date—7th year

52. *Outside the gate of the Asakusa Temple.* Part of a five-sheet print. Probably 1795.

53. *The third month on the Enoshima beach,*
from a set *The Elegant Amusements of the Four Seasons.* About 1796–8.

of Kansei, i.e. 1795, which is the date of the reconstruction of the Asakusa temple. If, as it is reasonable to suppose, this was a sort of commemorative print, then it could not have been issued much later than 1795.

Certainly, the drawing of the women in this print (Fig. 52) has all the characteristics that a study of other prints induces us to accept as belonging to the mid-nineties—elongated, willowy forms with distinctly long necks, and the beginnings of a hairstyle of which the main feature is a huge bulbous pile that balloons out at the back, assuming, as the century grows older, even larger and more extravagant forms.

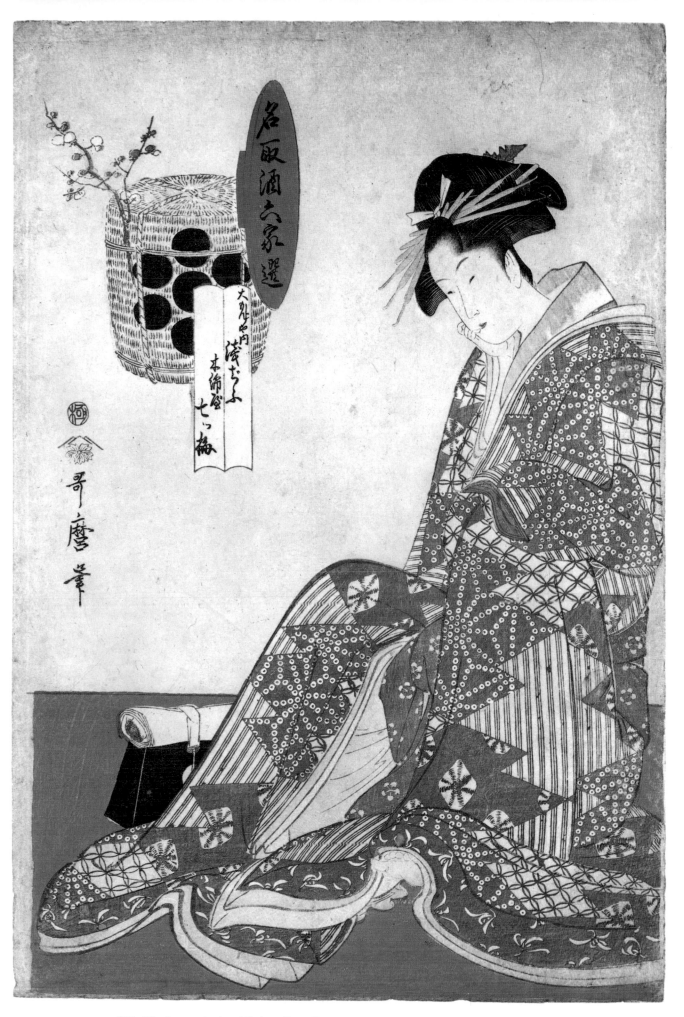

名取酒六家選

大見やり内 浅ぢぶ 本締窓 七ッ梅

IX. *The beauty Asajū of Daimonji-ya.* From the series *Natori Sake Rok'kasen.* 1792–4.
Boston, Mass., Museum of Fine Arts.

申
刻

青
樓
十
二
時

續

X. *The Hour of the Monkey [3–5 p.m.]*, from the series *The Twelve Hours of the Green Houses*. About 1795.

CHAPTER THIRTEEN

'THE TWELVE HOURS OF THE GREEN HOUSES'

ABOUT 1795, it is conjectured, Utamaro designed a set of prints that has become the focus of that form of criticism which strikes at him for the extremely attenuated non-naturalistic forms he gave to the women portrayed in his prints. It is a criticism never, I imagine, voiced in Japan, where any liberty with human and other natural forms is condoned in the cause of elegant design and pattern, but to Western appreciation, with its inherent bias towards simple representation, the arbitrary fashion in which the Japanese artists distort the female form has always been a stumbling block. Utamaro's series entitled *Seirō Jūni Toki Tsuzuki* (*'The Twelve Hours of the Green Houses'*) was undoubtedly one of his most splendidly produced sets, and one upon which he quite clearly exerted his mature powers to the utmost (Figs. 54, 55; Pl. X), so that its appearance presents opportunity to discuss the accusations of 'exaggeration' and 'deformity'.

Others have pointed out that the elongation of the human form has been a feature of the paintings of certain European artists—Pontormo and Poelenburgh being among those who have wilfully drawn out the figures from motives either of affectation or super-refinement, whereas El Greco and Blake created the abnormal under the stress of some inward compulsion that forced their lines into unnatural moulds, as a poet in a moment of intensest vision gives vent to 'whirling words'.

With Utamaro, two causes have been suggested for the gradual lengthening of the girls' forms from the unexceptional figure of the early eighties to the extreme height of this *Twelve Hours* set.

The first of these is almost a case for sociology—the suggestion that every Japanese woman, by nature inclined to be short and a little plump, aspires towards an impossible ideal of slender height (and let us not smile at this foible, for a glance at the advertisements of any of our houses of fashion shows that the woman of the West today sees herself with just such an attenuated slim form), so that, in depicting an ideal of elegance, Utamaro was simply following the vogue. This is an attractive hypothesis, but has, I believe, little foundation in fact. The second is far more to the point: the lengthening

of the figures gave opportunities for novel compositional effects, the contrast of the lines of a seated figure opposed to those of one standing beside, the swing of one form against another moving slightly in contrary direction, the wonderfully decorative effects of long sweeping lines of drapery, all being enhanced and given new potentialities by the exaggerated forms.

Kitao Masanobu in his seven diptychs comprising the *Mirror comparing the handwriting of the courtesans* had depicted girls of imposing stature, but Kiyonaga was the first to exploit to the full the possibilities of immensely tall types, in the statuesque processional groupings characteristic of him. Eishi, too, early followed the new mode and designed some sets of superbly posed single figures that seem to have had their effect on Utamaro. In this series, Utamaro confined himself to two or three figures, with a resource in composition that, like the score of a musician, reveals the true mastery of his medium.

Fenollosa extolled Kiyonaga's prints in which divinely tall girls appear, but in regard to Utamaro saw something quite sinister in the manifestation: 'Why the taste for distorted tallness in women's figures should have come at this date it is difficult to say . . . But it was no accident. Back of all outward demonstration lay a restlessness of this people who now, in their complete separation from the upper classes, felt that something more than a negativity of revolt was demanded, yet knew hardly where to look for a positive element to incorporate. The very plays had something seditious and threatening in their motives.'

Ukiyo-e art as the art of the people did naturally respond to the moods and to the tempo of the hour, and possibly the search for elegance verging on freakishness grew intenser as the century waned, Utamaro recording this phase as accurately as a finely-adjusted instrument. But it is to be remarked that the fashion for tallness which Kiyonaga had led died out before 1790, at which time he had reverted to a type nearer the norm, that same diminutive figure that charms us in Utamaro's prints of the period: and furthermore, it was only a passing phase with Utamaro too, who by 1800 was drawing figures that were probably tall by Japanese standards, but considerably less so than the girls in the *Twelve Hours* and in other sets produced at about the same time.

In the majority of the twelve prints of this set, I do not think one is conscious of any ‘distortion’ at all: one surrenders completely to the mastery of the design, the superbly rendered garments, the rare colours, and if occasionally, as perhaps in the *Hour of Midnight*, the proportions of the girls are disturbing in their exaggeration, the prints never merit Fenollosa’s sneer—‘The fabulous yards of dress goods required to clothe these giantesses gave Utamaro’s pen a magnificent opportunity of running away with itself and getting lost somewhere in the labyrinth of the skirts’—one is conscious the whole time of the artist’s absolute command of the design and the draughtsmanship is of the highest order throughout.

The sheets are superlatively printed, and inevitably raise again the question as to how much of their beauty depends on the craftsmen who engraved and printed the designs. Was it ultimately the printer who selected those exquisite tints, the result, it seems, of a search for the rare, broken or undecided colour—or was he closely supervised by the artist? So often the choice of colour seems to have been part of the original inspiration of the print that it is difficult to believe that two independent minds were responsible for the work, and I think that in such publishing houses as Tsutajū’s the printers were under continual supervision from the artists, who were responsible for the selection of the colours used—never quite the same when printed as the colours of the brush-artist, but possessing nuances of their own, and often a sort of glow or bloom, partly caused by the admixture of rice-paste to the printing colours, partly by the silky texture of the paper. Moreover, an added beauty is given to this series by the gold dust that is sprinkled over the yellow backgrounds, surrounding the colourful figures in a sort of lustrous vignette, in a technique reminiscent of the *Shell Book*, whose pages are similarly dusted with gold.

It is dubious whether the prints are meant to represent occupations of the courtesans traditionally associated with each hour. As so often, the title has a very tenuous connection with the subjects, at least to us, though it became a popular motive with Ukiyo-e artists, Utamaro himself producing other sets with the same title later.

The chief *raison d’être* for this set, as for others, may have been to display the latest fashion in dress. An artist’s popularity in Edo depended to some extent on his ability to depict the most fashionable and the most exclusive dresses, or even, perhaps, to create new models and novel patterns for fabrics. Just how close was this association in the public’s mind of the colour-prints with dress can be gathered from the fact that from the first, the colour-prints were known as *nishiki-e*, or ‘brocade pictures’. Utamaro actually designed prints advertising the creations of famous houses of fashion in Edo. To display the sumptuous garments to the best advantage, he did not hesitate to draw out his mannequins to impossible height just as our fashion artists do now. A glance at any gown-dealers’ advertisement in *Vogue* or *Harper’s Bazaar* will reveal Utamaro’s influence today.

Few of the artist’s patrons were, I feel sure, ever likely to wear such creations with such *élan*: they bought the prints as ideals of elegance with little more hope of emulation than the average typist or factory-hand has of emulating the models displaying Dior’s gowns pictured in the daily press. The historian who, one hundred and fifty years hence, conjures up a picture of the throng in a London street solely from the fashion plates in today’s stylish magazines will be no further from the truth than we are in recreating the teeming crowds of Edo from remembrance of Utamaro’s prints.

Did Utamaro actually design the dresses and perhaps more important, the patterns of the stuffs as well? Was he in fact Hartnell and Jacqmar at one and the same time? Or did he simply reproduce the creations of the great houses of fashion like Irakura, for whom he designed advertisements?

Brocades and silks, the range of colours and the inexhaustibly varied designs with which they were decorated, had always figured largely in the paintings and prints of the Ukiyo-e school, the insistence on such details of the ‘everyday’ world was one of the marks distinguishing these artists, and so closely did they follow the fashions of the day that it is possible roughly to date their productions by the kind of decoration in vogue. A great deal of the attractiveness of the prints lies in the exquisite drapery, the lovely colours and patterning of the stuffs, in which that outstanding gift of the Japanese for conventionalizing natural forms for ornamental design is seen at its best. It was just in this sphere

54. *The Hour of the Cock.* From the series *The Twelve Hours of the Green Houses.* About 1795.

55. *After the bath: The Hour of the Serpent [9–11 a.m.]*, from the series *The Twelve Hours of the Green Houses.*
About 1795.

that Utamaro excelled; his finest prints, as, for instance, in this series of *Twelve Hours of the Green Houses*, may justifiably be thought of as the apotheosis of the Japanese gown, and in my own mind I do not doubt that most of these creations were Utamaro's own. It would perhaps be an exercise in dress sense, though not one I have attempted, to try to distinguish between such contemporary artists as Utamaro and, say Eishi, by the predilection of one or the other for a certain cut or for a bias towards some distinctive colour scheme of floral decoration. Most of the prints we see have lost the startling brilliancy that once caught the eye of the Edo shopper as he or she passed the publisher's stalls. If we could think of their impact on the Edo public, we must revive the colours to their original vividness: then they fit better into one's picture of

the rather hectic world that Edo must have been, where lavish display more often than not cloaked a desperate poverty, and where the colourful processions of the Daimyōs and their retinues, or of the courtesans in the Yoshiwara streets, took place against so sombre a background. 'Of the magnificence that prevailed,' Murdoch wrote, 'a great deal was utterly insubstantial and factitious. Thousands of *hatamoto* and *samurai* had hopelessly outrun their means and were in debt. But appearances had to be kept up, a gay and gallant show maintained.' For anything like a just comparison to this superficial elegance at a time of general distress and squalor we have to go to eighteenth-century France, the France, indeed, of Utamaro's own time. The comparison between Paris and Edo, the 'Paris of the East', was never closer than at this time.

CHAPTER FOURTEEN

UTAMARO IN MIDDLE LIFE

THOUGH WE ARE able to place Utamaro's works in something near chronological order, facts concerning his life during these middle years are almost entirely lacking. The *Twelve Hours* bring us, however, to what might be called the 'central legend' of Utamaro's life—his drunkenness and debauchery.

The accusations seem to have been built up on the dark hints of native biographies that have been proved unreliable in many instances, and without corroboration can only be accepted with reserve: their testimony is little better than unsubstantiated rumour. However, that is not to deny that Utamaro belonged to the 'fast set' of Edo—it is highly probable that he did: wine-bibbing and wenching seem to have been accepted among his class as peccadilloes, and there is every reason to suspect that he did his share of both. But if there is no smoke without fire, it is also true that quite moderate fires can cause a great deal of smoke.

Once European writers had discovered the germ of the legend, having very little other biographical data from which to spin out an account of his life, they fostered it to such an extent that when eventually J. J. O'Brien Sexton began to throw doubts upon the twisted plant that had sprung from this dubious seed, the roots were so deep that he was unable to grub it up and indeed, though shaken, it still flourishes. As I have said, the growth of the legend took place in Europe. How did it all start?

56. *The foyer of a theatre.* Frontispiece to a book entitled *Yakusha Gaku Tsū.* 1799.

57. *The fowler.*

Ultimately, to explain that properly, one would need to analyse the extraordinarily complex mind of Edmond de Goncourt, subtle, sensuous, sensitive to every new artistic manifestation, who wrote

'Mais, il y a un tel charme à travailler dans du *neuf*, sur des êtres et des objets, où vous ne rencontrez pas en avant de vous, un, deux, trois et même dix précurseurs!' But with a faculty for sensing the new went a tendency to seek in it characteristics that were sympathetic to his own temperament, with its ultra-Parisian culture and preoccupation with the abnormal, the piquantly perverted. De Goncourt was a novelist at a period when, to be interesting, a character had to have a streak of wickedness and a tendency towards the obscurer vices: the archetype of these unpleasant heroes being Essaintes in Huysmans' *A Rebours*. Utamaro's art became the more exciting if it were considered to be the work of a man who interrupted his debauchery in the licensed quarter to dash off a dozen 'or so designs for the clamouring publishers. Something of the same *succès de scandale* has popularized the work of such artists as Toulouse-Lautrec and Gauguin.

The very subtitle of de Goncourt's book, *Outamaro: Le Peintre des Maisons Vertes*, was calculated to give a one-sided impression, suggesting that the 'Green Houses' were Utamaro's sole interest—far from the truth, as I think I have shown. What I look on as the very first burgeoning of the legend occurs in a passage in this book:

'Long before I knew that Utamaro was a sort of official painter of the Yoshiwara, one day, turning over, with Hayashi, the set of the "Twelve Hours",[1] with the sixth plate in front of me, representing that girl rather graciously tall, dressed in a pale robe starred with a star-fish design, of a frail blue as though drowned in water, that girl, to whom a little kneeling *musume* offers a cup of tea, and whose slight neck, the upper part of a shoulder voluptuously thin from consumption, and a little pointed breast, are bared by the falling dress (Fig. 55), I said to Hayashi:

"The man that drew that girl came to be a lover of the female form?"

"You are right," replied Hayashi, "he died of exhaustion."'

And in another passage he lays down the lines on which most subsequent writers have proceeded in dealing with Utamaro's life:

'According to the biographers,' he wrote, 'Utamaro's life is quite regular: the day he passes with his publisher Tsutaya Jūsaburō, with whom he had a studio; the night he passes at the Yoshiwara. And it is not far from the studio to the Green Houses,

[1]Described in the last chapter.

since the house of the publisher adjoins the portals of the Yoshiwara. This explains the artist's profound knowledge of the "Flowery Quarter".'

If Utamaro had been alone in seeking so much of his material within the Yoshiwara there might have been reason to suppose him obsessed with the pleasures to be found there, but it is now generally accepted that it was a rendezvous for many artists and authors who visited it for the purpose of obtaining 'copy', or for the company that foregathered there, or as much from curiosity as for the favours of the courtesans. Jippensha Ikku, who wrote the text of the *Annals of the Green Houses* of 1804 says in his introduction: 'This book is the outcome of what I have heard and seen these many years past', and later tells how he 'peeped through every hole he could find in the sliding walls so as accurately to spy out the rules and customs of each particular house'. And Ikku was only one of a number.

The role that has been assigned by some to the courtesans, as the *hetaerae* of a romantic underworld where political and other refugees found asylum, is probably hardly in keeping with the facts; but that there was a ferment of new ideas, and a stirring of unrest, however slight, a premonitory tremor of the disintegration of a society that in fundamentals had been unchanged for centuries, and that this stirring and ferment were sensed more than elsewhere in places like the Yoshiwara and the tea-houses frequented by the intelligentsia, is scarcely open to doubt. There was something in the atmosphere of the time that had its effect upon Utamaro's work, observable not so much in any change of subject-matter as in a more febrile design, a slackening of the rein, a lowering of the high and exacting standards he had hitherto maintained. Naturally, these effects were gradual and probably account only in part for the deterioration in Utamaro's work at the turn of the century—dissipation may have been a contributory cause.

For he was, after all, a true child of his times, with the same struggle during lean years as other commoners in Edo, the same tendency to apply to the bottle and other forms of oblivion as they, and whose familiarity with the interior of the Yoshiwara was, we may be sure, not simply the result of a search for 'copy'. The band of writers and artists who gathered round the enlightened publisher Tsutajū formed a clique that represented the *avant-garde* of the Ukiyo-e world and a little Bohemia of its own. The

58. *The lovers Oshichi and Kichisaburō.*

59. From the series *Love scenes represented by Marionettes*. About 1801.

novelist Jippensha Ikku, creator of the funniest book in the Japanese language, the *Hizakurige;* the other genius Kitao Masanobu; the novelist Bakin; the comic poets Shoku-sanjin, Kankō and Sanna; Chōki and the enigmatic Sharaku—all these and more were the dependants, *kakari-bito*, of Tsutajū, and if they did not live under the same roof, must often have been in each other's company. Practically nothing is known of Chōki or Sharaku, but Masanobu and Ikku have both earned reputations —whether justly or not I cannot say—for dissoluteness, and both were much in Utamaro's company. Certainly there was nothing puritanical in Utamaro's companions; they were, and I think Utamaro was

60. *Girl applying cosmetic to her neck.* About 1796.

61. *Hawk on a plum-branch*. About 1798.

of their number, the sophisticated wits of their day.

In 1797, Tsutajū died. His publisher, friend and probably guide of over twenty years' standing, whose house he had shared since the earliest days of his print-designing, Utamaro must have felt his loss keenly. Indeed, it is perhaps not far from the truth to look on the ending of an association that always seems to have conduced to Utamaro's well-being as the removal of a stabilizing influence, as a loss that contributed, like the atmosphere of the time, to the breaking down of standards both of conduct and artistic effort.

Shortly after this event, Utamaro is thought to have married. Most native records agree on this, and though Bakin, a contemporary, averred that Utamaro had neither wife nor child, there are sufficient scraps of corroborative evidence to make it a matter almost of certainty. Marriage among men and women of Utamaro's class was a rather

business-like arrangement, the engagement of a housekeeper, child-bearer and nurse. Although women were considerably more free and uninhibited in Japan than in many other parts of the East, their relationship with their husbands rarely rose above that of a servant to a master: devotion and obedience were more than mere marriage promises, they were given unquestioningly by the wife. This relationship, the accepted inferiority of one party, shows how misleading the term 'wife' can be with its immediate European connotation: in Japan another word was used with different meanings. Yet the one memorial we have of Utamaro's wife, if one could believe it authentic, shows her in the happiest accord with her husband, sharing in fact, in his work. The preface to one of Utamaro's erotic books, undated but belonging to the last years of the century, the *Ehon Warai Jōgo* (literally '*Laughing Drunkards*'), purports to be written by no other than this lady.

Utamaro's erotica have already been dealt with and there is no need here to say more than that the contents of *Ehon Warai Jōgo* are hardly the sort of thing a 'lady' would confess to knowing at all. But here is the letter to the publisher translated from the preface to the book:

'Herewith, right honourable sir, I wish to say that in spite of the continuing cold weather, your worthy relationship is well and in good humour, and I also express the most fervent wish that it is the same with you.

'My man Maro has been summoned by a distinguished acquaintance and must make a journey to Enoshima suddenly. On that account, this enclosed book of pictures I send is coloured by me, although I am not as skilful as he is. The work is highly embarrassing for a lady, but I am after all the wife of an artist, and "The devil's wife is also a wicked spirit". So it comes about in these circumstances that night after night as a grass widow I laboured at this night work. In truth, many blunders have crept into it which will not please you, but think what a happily loving couple we are and now, by this means, with the husband making the designs and the wife colouring them, an intimate union of a male and female has come about that harmonizes excellently with the drift of the picture book. Therefore you will be able to sell it well. In spite of sedulous reflection, I have had no happy idea for the title of the book. I have called it after my own temperament "Laughing Drunkards". Finally I beseech you to publish it in a quite complete state.

Best Wishes.'

It is more than likely, however, that this letter is a fiction and that the publisher to whom the letter is addressed "Mr Matsu-midori-ya" hoped to add to the flavour of the book by arranging for a woman to introduce the erotic pictures. The book is not signed by the artist, but if the 'Maro' mentioned in the introduction was as plainly 'Utamaro' as it is to us, the Edo readers would have quite appreciated the joke of the introduction, even if they sensed that it could not have been written by his wife, or even, again, if they knew he had no wife: to credit the artist with a fictitious wife, especially one of the calibre indicated in her letter, would be quite in the vein of this type of book.

There is no record of any children, but doubtless there was issue, and it is perhaps significant that in the following years some of Utamaro's finest prints depict mother and child in a multitude of accurately observed poses, the famous series of *Yama-Uba and Kintoki* being only an extension of the same theme.

Utamaro was outlived by his wife, who, after his death, married his pupil, Koikawa Yukimachi, or Baigadō Utamaro II as he became known, and who seems to have taken over Utamaro's signature as part of the marriage settlement.

It is to him, and other unscrupulous appropriators of the real Utamaro's signature, that many of the feeblest prints bearing the signature can safely be assigned. Where they bear a year-seal subsequent to that of Utamaro's death (1806) they can be dismissed with certainty: concerning some of the remainder, there are often doubts, and it is probably unfair to father on to his followers all the inferior prints of Utamaro's last years. They are, in any case, an inconsiderable body of prints, and whether we give them to Utamaro or to his plagiarists neither adds nor detracts from his stature.

62. *Theatrical duo*. A fan-print. About 1798–1800.

CHAPTER FIFTEEN

THE SETS OF 'RENOWNED LOVERS' AND OTHER PRINTS

1795–1800

IN THESE YEARS, we witness both the climax of Utamaro's originality as a print-designer, and the beginning of a descent from the pinnacle of his powers. It is the period of what may be regarded as the central series of prints in his mature and most personal style, furthest from Kiyonaga and other early influences and from the vulgarized parodies of himself found in Eizan and other late plagiarists: the prints which Fenollosa probably thought of as the 'most Utamaro-ish in Utamaro'. His inventiveness and resource in seeking out new subjects and fresh technical expedients was never higher; his innovations in the compositions involving half- or three-quarter-length figures are the cause today of the widest admiration; the woman of the prints becomes, if anything, more alluring, despite a more obvious mannerism in the treatment of her form.

A glance at the reproduction of one sheet of the *Firefly* triptych (Fig. 63) will show the features that characterize this exquisitely mannered form—the slender height, the narrow oval face, the long neck tapering from the shoulder up to the chin. The charges of 'unnaturalism' invariably sound most convincing when such prints as this are analysed and the length of the head, and the proportion of the head to the body, worked out in mathematical equations, but as I have pointed out, Utamaro had other aims than simple representation.

But before going on to the period to which the *Firefly* triptych properly belongs, there are earlier prints that merit attention.

First, linking the early three-quarter length portraits with the *Large Heads* soon to be described, is a very impressive series *Tōji zensei bijin zoro-e* ('*Flourishing Beauties of the Present Day*'). This is another series of courtesans in which Utamaro still plays the 'physiognomist': but already a difference is noticeable in the characterization of the girls he depicts (Fig. 64). There is something restless, as if from frustration, suppressed desire, or *ennui* in the attitudes and gestures of these girls. One thrusts her arms before her, fingers convulsively locked and ex-

pressing the very despair of longing; another kneels in an attitude that might be of prayer, her fan dangling from her supplicating clasped hands; another grips her writing brush in her teeth as she unrolls the paper for a letter that her expression tells must be portentous; a fourth screws up a letter she has just read, and though her face is emotionless, the hands and arms are eloquent of exasperation and anger. There is a dynamism in these portraits, a latent power that is intense even by Utamaro's standards, and the gorgeous robes and the large scale of the figures imposingly filling the sheets make the set a memorable one.

A triptych entitled *Fujin tomari kyaku no zu* ('*A picture of fair sojourners at an inn*') conveys a sense of some underlying emotion beneath the calm un-eventfulness of the action. Nothing more enchanting than this print (Fig. 65) exists in Utamaro's *œuvre*. Noguchi, one of those Japanese writers who have endeavoured to interpret the art of his countrymen to the Western world, has written of the deep impression this triptych made upon him when he first saw it (in the British Museum!). 'Here is mood in the colour,' he writes (his English is uncertain), 'strangely opening to a charming vista of dream hitherto unknown in the West.' It is indeed to a dreamlike world that this print transports us, though it is a matter-of-fact scene it represents: women preparing their mosquito net before retiring to bed. Three are within the net, seated among rich quilts, and outside stand three tall and unimaginably lovely girls, one in the act of securing, with a movement of Grecian grace, a corner of the net, another pensively untying her girdle, a third folding up a transparent garment through which her frail arms are visible.

The treatment of the net is a technical triumph, the green gauze seems to shed a faint green shadow over the girls within as if they were viewed through still water, and the result is an enchanting fusion of nameless colours; the net's long lines stretch across the three sections of the print and link the groups in a most natural way. And more than that: the penumbra in which these seated girls are half-obscured suggests the borderline of sleep, across which they dreamily watch their companions and communicate to us the hush of a midsummer night, the perfumed privacy of a room in an inn in some country as remote from us as Babylon.

Another print, somewhat later, in which this net motif is employed with telling effect is that of a young man, inside the net, reclining on his elbows and affectedly puffing at his pipe, whilst his fair companion of the night lifts the lower edge of the net and prepares to emerge. All that lies beyond the gauze is in subdued colour, but, lifting the edge, the girl seems to come out into the blaze of morning sunshine, causing her to screw up her eyes, flooding this part of the picture with bright purples and reds of her dresses, and accentuating the whiteness of her face and arms (Fig. 66).

64. *The courtesan Morokoshi of the Echizen House*, from the set *Flourishing Beauties of the Present Day*. 1795–7.

It has been suggested that fine muslin was actually used by the printer to secure the delicate lines of the net in these prints and others where the mosquito net appears. Utamaro was continually introducing novel effects in the way of printing and engraving. In one set *Musume Hi-dokei* ('*Daily Occupations of Young Women*') the faces are printed without a key-block and simply left white against a darker background. He delighted in employing the printer's art to depict filmy, semi-transparent stuffs, suggesting the thinness of the material by a change of colour in the dress seen beneath, or (as in the *Flourishing Beauties of the Present Day* series) by deepening the colours of the transparent robe at the folds. Another novelty was the use of a red instead of a black outline, or key-block, for faces and other exposed parts of the body, an artifice that is a feature of certain of the set of prints *New Pattern of Brocade* and a number of the

63. *Firefly catching, a summer pastime.*
One sheet of a triptych. About 1796–7.

Large Heads that are described later; and in a series of bust portraits representing the six Tamagawa, the backgrounds are completely patterned with a blind-printed design, one, for instance, with the conventionalized 'river' motif, another with pine needles, flowers and the *kinuta* used for beating linen when fulling.

Another innovation brings me back to the last phase of the reign of tall women in Utamaro's art. The print called *Above and below Ryōgoku Bridge* is designed as two triptychs, one to fit *above* the other, a most uncommon format, though Toyokuni repeated it in a theatrical print later. But the device is a questionable one, for though the Japanese artists' skill was equal to designing three or more sheets laterally, maintaining at the same time a sense of completeness in each component part, it was unable to succeed when the division was a vertical one. Hence these two triptychs are best, to my mind, considered separately. And what superb prints they are!

In *Above the Bridge*, there is a *Frieze of Girls* who, as if in procession, have stopped to watch the comings and goings of boats plying on the Sumida below (Fig. 67). The connecting link (serving the same purpose as the lines of the mosquito net in *Fair sojourners at an inn*) is the stout wooden balustrade of the bridge; its bold squareness makes the perfect foil to the flowing curves of the promenaders.

Below the Bridge is another cleverly composed scene. We are almost beneath the Ryōgoku, passing between its immense piles, through which we have a view down the river, the green banks converging at the distant horizon at a point where it is spanned by another of the Edo wooden bridges. Like those watching them above, the girls in the boats are in their most fashionable clothes. One, fan in teeth, is passing from one boat to another, gracefully assisted by a friend who steadies the prow of the boat she is leaving and catches her wrist. The *sake* cup awaits her in the hands of another girl seated in the boat, and a third lifts the *sake* kettle in readiness for her coming. There is all the *bonhomie* of warm carefree days of idleness in this print.

The *Firefly* triptych depicts a scene often favoured by the popular school: girls and young children endeavouring to capture fireflies at night-time, indicated in this print by the dark grey band of sky at the top edge of the print (Fig. 63). Another triptych of this time is a nightpiece with fireworks

65. *Fair sojourners at an inn.* Triptych. About 1796.

on the river, also a favourite summertime attraction of the town. Under a sky strewn with stars, the Ryōgoku Bridge is black with sightseers, dark grey silhouettes of boats are dotted about the gleaming river, an enormous serpent-like flame coils up into the sky from a firework held by a man discerned at the prow of one of the boats. The foreground figures are picked out in bright colours and in white against a dark grey ground that without banks or boundary merges with the river and symbolizes night. The same tall figures are repeated in another piece of this time depicting girls among the irises in the famous garden of Horikiri.

But perhaps the most extreme manifestation of this phase of exaggeratedly tall forms comes in a print (Pl. XI) which enables one to judge how great

a distance had been travelled since the *Women preparing stuff for dresses* of about 1794, discussed in Chapter XII, how the tall but solid forms of that print have become attenuated, etherealized to a degree that bespeaks an enormous change in the artist's style in the four or five years that have elapsed. This is an outdoor scene, girls in a garden where a broad length of silk has been hung out to dry, one end attached to a tree at the right-hand side of the picture, the other to the corner of the house at the extreme left.

We have in this print the very ecstasy of extravagance in form, and from another hand it might have seemed morbid distortion, but the dresses are so lovely, the attitudinizing so exquisitely artificial (Watteau's simpering creatures are not more mannered), the by-play of the figures so engaging, that we succumb entirely to the artist's magic.

These prints seem to mark the culmination of the fashion for extreme height and slenderness, and gradually there is a return, if not to the normal form, at least to one less removed from it; by 1800, the tall haunting beauty of the *Twelve Hours* and the *Frieze of Girls* has been forsaken and does not appear again. One certain date of this period is the publication date, 1798, of an album entitled *Otoka doka*, the name of a dance performed by men. Of the six plates comprising the album, Utamaro contributed one, in company with Eishi, Shigemasa, Hokusai, and two others less well-known. In this print (Fig. 68) the girls are of unremarkable stature, and even making allowance for the different style

66. *Girl emerging from mosquito-net, watched by her lover.* About 1799.

XI. *Girls drying a length of silk in a garden.* From a triptych. About 1797–8.

XII. From *New Patterns of Brocade after Utamaro's Style*. 1797–8.

67. *Above the Ryōgoku Bridge.* Triptych. About 1796–8.

that was often employed in album work, it seems reasonable to infer that the vogue for tallness had already had its day.

We come now to one of the 'key' sets of prints of this transitional period of Utamaro's career—that entitled *Nishiki-ori Utamaro gata shin mōyō* ('*New Patterns of Brocade after Utamaro's style*'), published by Tsuruya, of which three prints are known. What occasioned the issue of these prints in 1797 or 1798, whether Utamaro was suffering under the slight received at a rival's hand or whether he was impelled by a genuine indignation at the shoddy work that was by now appearing in the print shops, we are never likely to know, but these splendid designs were of an order to put all competitors to rout, and bear challenging inscriptions that are of significance in throwing light on the artist's view of his contemporaries, and in bringing home to us his pride in the standard of his own productions. Each is the picture of a single girl in sumptuous brocade, depicted against a yellow background without the use of a key-block outline, save only for the face, arms and hands, for which a red outline was used in two instances. That he meant to dazzle the public with these superbly produced prints and to command attention by their unusual devices is obvious, and it is the more curious that so few have survived: all three prints are extremely rare.

The first, one of the best known of all Utamaro's prints, is of a kneeling courtesan drawing her robe together in front of her body and turning her head as she looks back over her shoulder (Pl. XII). The folds of the white outer garment are indicated with sweeping brushstrokes, wonderfully reproduced by the colour-printer, whose graded colour without outline looks exactly like a watercolour wash. The hair is finely engraved, always a mark of *de luxe* in a print of this period. The inscription runs as follows: 'If power be in the brush, though the painting of a pretty face be roughly sketched and merely in ink, yet the living stroke of my brush will create a Seishi (Chinese beauty). Another man may paint a plain woman with powdered face and in gorgeous costume but the painting itself being poor loses its colour and gradually reveals its want of proportion. My fee for drawing is as high as my nose.[1] Low street-girls are cheap in comparison with *oiran* of a thousand yen. Publishers who buy cheap must take the consequences, their proud noses will be crushed.'[2]

The second print is of another kneeling girl supporting herself on one arm as she reads a letter spread out upon her thighs and holding in her right hand a tobacco pipe (Fig. 69). 'Here is a specimen,' runs the inscription, 'of *nishiki-e* of Azuma (Edo). Recently, there have appeared wretched prints, made by daubers who, day after day, swarm like

[1] This is a Japanese expression meaning 'as great as my pride'. So, too, the publishers' pride would be humbled.
[2] Translated in the British Museum Catalogue.

68. A page from the album *Otoka-doka*, 1798, to which Eishi, Shigemasa and Hokusai also contributed.

ants. These prints, which pretend to imitate the style of the masters, are stupidly designed and hideously coloured. They compromise the reputation of the true *nishiki-e*, not only in Japan, but also among foreigners. The present series of prints is designed to discourage, or otherwise to teach a lesson to, these imitators.'

Lastly, there is a print of a seated girl in a flowered dress which she is drawing over a scarlet undergarment. She has a black sash with a green pattern, and carries a fan with a red design. In the inscription, Utamaro is still harping on his prowess as 'physiognomist': 'There are only two ways of drawing beautiful women: one is to delineate the features, the other to expess the physiognomy. If, therefore, one draws a smiling face comprehensive of love, the person looking at the picture becomes excited, and if to this is added a delicate and graceful form, he becomes infatuated. I want all ladies and gentlemen to offer their criticisms only after they have scrutinized my elegant style and compared it with the deformities of others.'[3]

Nobody reading these inscriptions could be under

any doubt as to Utamaro's pride and sense of accomplishment, and from them too, we can deduce that irascibility and intolerance which no doubt went hand in glove with the pride and made him, like Whistler, a 'difficult' character to work with.

In these three prints, it is as much the technical virtuosity that impresses us as the designs themselves, which can at least be matched in other sets. But about the same time or shortly after, Utamaro made the designs for a number of sets that I have already spoken of as the most personal in style, the most inimitable of any in his *œuvre*. Two of the sets bear titles that have never satisfactorily been explained,[4] and both are concerned with 'renowned lovers', one being confined to the two figures, the other to the lovers and a third person in some way connected with their stories. *Ōmi Hakkei* is a set of pairs of lovers personifying the *Eight Views of Ōmi* (a quaint conceit dealt with in the next chapter); another is entitled *Fujin tewaza juni kō* ('*Twelve Forms of Women's Handiwork*'), each print

[3]Binyon and Sexton: *Japanese Colour Prints*.

[4]*Chiwa kagami tsuki no mura-kumo*. One translation is 'A mirror of flirting lovers: clusters of clouds across the moon'; and *Jitsu kurabe iro no minakami* 'An array of passionate lovers'.

69. From *New Patterns of Brocade after Utamaro's Style*. 1797–8.

depicting two girls engaged in some occupation, weaving, or hairdressing, or the like (Figs. 70, 71).

There had been many earlier sets in which the arrangement of two or three figures had pre-occupied Utamaro: the *Mu Tamagawa* (Fig. 50), and the *Twelve Hours* (Figs. 54, 55) for example: but in these later prints, Utamaro evolved his most personal treatment of the theme. Generally the figures are half- or three-quarter length, though the variation in the entry of each figure into the framework of the print constitutes one of the elements in the artist's power to surprise us. The figures are of large size and dominate the page, backgrounds being unimportant or non-existent. A new problem in composition was wilfully set by each successive print, and in most instances triumphantly solved. They are without a counterpart in the Japanese art up to that time, and few artists succeeded later in producing anything comparable. (Eisui, a pupil of Eishi, came nearest in one or two sets produced soon after Utamaro's).

It is as hard to analyse the pleasure these designs give as it is to explain why some arrangements of musical notes give more pleasure than others. The gift for spatial design shown in these prints is as unaccountable as a musician's gift for melody, and our response to the one as to the other is involuntary and unreasoning. Prints like *La Sortie* (Pl. XIII) or *O-ume and Kumenosuke* (Fig. 74) are not only the most 'Utamaro-ish' of prints, they epitomize for many the essential Japanese print. It was this type of composition, and the other relying upon a single large-scale head, that in the last century immediately appealed to the French Impressionists, who, probing beyond the existing limitations of Western design, found both an answer and an inspiration in the prints of Utamaro.

The heads designed on a large scale just mentioned also appeared during the late nineties. These prints, in which the head and neck take up the whole area of the print, are generally known as the *Large Heads*. They extend over the years 1796 to 1800 and exist in considerable numbers, so that they are apt to predominate in some collections, giving a wrong impression of their relative importance in Utamaro's output (Figs. 73, 75).

This type of print was not altogether new, Shunei before 1790, Utamaro himself shortly after, and Sharaku in 1794 having already developed the 'portrait' head. In this enlarged form, a greater strain is placed upon our powers of acceptance of the 'non-representational' portrait: whereas with the three-quarter-length studies it is easy to accept the conventions because the face is but one element of the design, the absence of characterization in a 'close-up', such as these heads are in effect, leads us to notice the blankness of the features. An enlargement of the conventional features, the narrow eyes, 'key-like' nose, the half-opened lips, succeeds only in making their emptiness more apparent, gives the faces an expression of insipidity or even vacuity which we find difficult to disregard. In contrast to the emptiness of the girls' features is the detailed treatment of the hair, forced by pieces of metal into devious shapes and mounted with a formidable array of pins and combs: instead of portraits, it might be complained that they are still-life arrangements of fantastic wigs mounted upon a hairdresser's dummy heads.

Nevertheless, we are constantly being surprised by the grandeur of some of these designs, composed of the bold mass of comb-bedizened black hair, the touch of bright colour at the neck of the dress, the suave lines of the oval face. Perhaps the large numbers that exist of this type of print may be due to this being the easiest of Utamaro's work to imitate, and many accepted as Utamaro's may be contemporary forgeries. That this is likely is borne out by the fact that several are signed with the prefix *Shōmei* to the artist's signature, signifying 'the true', 'the genuine' Utamaro.

Of these latter, a series by which the whole group can be typified has the title of *Seirō Nana Komachi* ('*Seven Komachi of the Green House*').[1] A feature of these prints is the care with which the hair is drawn and engraved, with the stray wisp falling out of place with the purpose, almost, of calling attention to the printer's and engraver's dexterity, as Giovanni Bellini called attention to his skill with the brush by laying on hair-fine brushstrokes. In contrast, the folds of the stuffs, as one raises her starfish-patterned towel to wipe an ear, or as another lifts her hands inside her sleeves, are given with broad sweeping lines that give an added frailty to the appearance of the outlines of the features and the minute hairs at the scalp.

By the late nineties, Utamaro had reached the zenith of his popularity. His designs were sought by practically every publisher of note, and series

[1]A title explained in Chapter XVII.

70. From *The Famous Eight Views of Ōmi*, each connected with a pair of lovers, in this case Umegawa and Chūbei. About 1797.

71. *Girl dressing a companion's hair.* From the series *Twelve Forms of Women's Handiwork*. About 1797–8.

72. *Saizaburō dressing the hair of Jōhachi, and O'koma looking on.* From *The Mirror of Flirting Lovers.* About 1797–8.

73. *Nan-eki, the Beauty of the South.* About 1797.

followed series, triptych followed triptych, at a pace that could not but impair the quality of the drawing, and that had its effect on the engravers and printers struggling to keep abreast with the public's overwhelming demand for *nishiki-e*. If it was difficult to chronicle fully the work of the earlier years, it is quite impossible to do anything like justice to the plethora of prints now issued. Some are described in this and in ensuing chapters, but many exist in public and private collections that not even Kurth or Yoshida catalogued and for which space does not allow mention.

One triptych, however, of the last years of the century must be given a place of honour here, as in every other notice of Utamaro's work—the *Awabi Fishers* (Pl. XIV).

This triptych, as rare as it is famous, is one of the strangest and most compelling of all the artist's countless works. The subject is not an unusual one: the diving-girls for the large scallop-like shellfish called *awabi* were almost a race apart among the Japanese, and pictures of them in the prints of the Ukiyo-e artists were popular in Edo. They appear in Utamaro's own work a number of times, in the *Uta-makura* print and in the early triptych referred to in Chapters VII and IX, and in a six-sheet print

XIII. *The lovers Koharu and Kamiya Jihei—the elopement known as 'La Sortie'*, from the series
An Array of Passionate Lovers. 1797–8.

XIV. *The Awabi Fishers*. From a triptych. About 1798.

74. *The lovers O-ume and Kumenosuke,* from the series *An Array of Passionate Lovers.* About 1797–8.

75. *Mother and Daughter*. About 1798–1800.

of small size dating from Utamaro's last years, *Awabi fishers off Enoshima beach*.

Of an everyday happening, Utamaro has made a masterpiece—and how unlike the triptych of ten years earlier, so beautiful also in *its* way. Gone are the effects of dainty pattern and varied colour, the mincing gait, the vivacious movement: instead, we have elemental forms that in pose and gesture belong to the age of Titans—their remoteness from the fashionable *Edo* world is made manifest by the intrusion of the city-clad woman with hair dressed

à la mode, whose contrast with the ponderous half-nude figures is one of Utamaro's masterstrokes.

There has been some controversy over the dating of this print but the coiffure of the Edo girl buying *awabi* marks it as belonging to the last two or three years of the century, and the semi-nude forms have a kinship with figures in the erotic albums of the same period. It is perhaps the last outstanding masterpiece of Utamaro's life: henceforward there was to be no dearth of good prints, but none quite of this calibre.

CHAPTER SIXTEEN

TRAVESTIES, PARODIES AND BURLESQUES

ONE OF THE features distinguishing the Ukiyo-e artists, and no doubt partly responsible for their low esteem in the view of the members of the old academies, was the appropriation, with a cavalier disregard for their sanctity, of subjects hallowed from antiquity. Classic subjects which, through literature and paintings, were familiar to the cultured middle and artisan classes of Edo, were treated with a genial playfulness, ranging from frank travesty, in which great characters of fiction and history enact little domestic dramas, to subtle allusion that called for an acute perceptiveness on the part of the beholder.

77. 'At the general request, Utamaro here depicts his gracious portrait', enacting a quite fanciful scene, with Yoshiwara girls, from the *Chūshingura*. About 1797–9.

76. A skit on the last scene of the *Chūshingura*. About 1800.

Not content with their role as 'painters of the passing show', they had to give the classics in modern dress, with just that note of incongruity we find in Shakespeare presented by actors in lounge suits against a background of a cocktail bar. Of course, this incongruity does not come home to us with the force it did to the Japanese of the day, for to us the dress and customs of Kyōto in the middle ages and of Edo in the eighteenth century are alike strange, and until we have learned to distinguish the dress and manners of the various periods of Japanese history, we are hardly likely to realize how

78. *The 'Niwaka festival'.* About 1793–5.

startling it must have been to the Japanese that the famous medieval poets should appear in brocade of the most up-to-date pattern, or that Prince Genji, hero of the eleventh-century romance, should carry on his amours in a modern Edo tea-house, with geisha and courtesans from the Yoshiwara as his companions.

It follows that this quality of gentle parody is the Ukiyo-e characteristic last to be appreciated by Western admirers, and in fact, owing to its semi-literary basis, it is one we only partially apprehend at best. Without a knowledge of the legends, stories, poems, historical and religious events so whimsically garbled, many of the titles of the sets of prints are quite meaningless, and without the right clues, the *double-entendres* of the pictures are lost.

79. *Three geisha girls performing in the Niwaka festival*, when the visit of the Korean ambassador was parodied (hence the conical hat). One of the early series on mica ground. About 1792-4.

As often as not, some hint of the by-play is given by the word *fūryū* appearing as the first word in the cartouche bearing the title of a print or set of prints. *Fūryū* is composed of two characters signifying *à la mode*, 'up-to-date' or 'elegant' in the sense of being fashionable. Thus, for example, the title *Fūryū Nana Komachi* meant the 'Seven Scenes of Komachi up-to-date', and from the earliest Ukiyo-e artists

onwards, under this or a similar title had been presented a travesty of the seven traditional scenes in the life of the famous medieval poetess Komachi.

Utamaro designed a number of sets of prints based on the *Seven Komachi* scenes, and in some, as the set of *Large Heads* referred to in the last chapter, the allusions are so recondite as completely to escape the foreigner, though to the

80. *Evening Snow*, from the *Eight Views of Biwa*.
About 1798–1800.

Japanese, steeped in Komachi's poetry, the allusions may have been plain enough.

Perhaps the Japanese story best known outside the country is that of the *Chūshingura* or 'Loyal League', commonly known as the 'Forty-seven *Rōnin*'. Founded on an historical event of the eighteenth century, it was dramatized soon after and became the most popular of all the national stories and plays, the action of the *samurai* in revenging the insult to their lord, forced to forfeit his life for a blow aimed at a courtier who had provoked him beyond endurance, becoming the type and exemplar of courage and loyalty, traits that appealed to something deep in the Japanese character. Depictions of the eleven scenes of the play founded upon the history were made by nearly all the leading Ukiyo-e artists, and the sequence of events and the characters taking part took on a 'traditional' aspect.

Even of this favourite play, Utamaro made a number of burlesques, drawing comparisons between the scenes of the play and some everyday

affair of an Edo household, parodying the noble ferocity and derring-do of the Forty-seven *Rōnin* in the mimic battles of children at play, and, in his best known set of this kind, giving all the parts to women, and in the rites and pleasures of the Yoshiwara, the intrigues and petty squabbles of the 'violets', suggesting distant parallels to the familiar actions of the drama. To illustrate these odd metamorphoses in detail would require a thorough exposition of the play, not possible here, but the oblique methods of the artist can be shown by reference to a single scene.

In the play, Moronao, by his insulting behaviour, goads Enya to attack him, but Honzō, fearing the consequences, tries to restrain his master Enya. In the *Chūshingura in Daily Life* series, this scene is represented by a husband attacking a nagging wife with a pestle, whilst a woman arrests his arm, and a man sets on him from the rear. In *The Loyal League compared to Children's Amusements*, the performers are children: one boy is restraining his baby brother, who, armed with a drumstick, is attacking another lad sprawled on the floor. Finally, in the *Comparison of Celebrated Beauties and the Loyal League*, Hishiya, a courtesan armed with a rolled up towel is about to set upon another, Takashima, seated unsuspectingly on the ground, but a *kamuro* throws herself between the two. An interesting, but uncorroborated, theory regarding this set, which comes from the mid-nineties and has in its eleventh scene a self-portrait of Utamaro (Fig. 77), was propounded by Théodore Duret in the *Art Journal*. He stated that one particular version of the Chūshingura was 'performed by a company consisting exclusively of actresses, contrary to the general custom of the Japanese stage, by which all the characters, both men and women, are impersonated by men. Utamaro was probably intimately associated with the leading members of the troupe and portrayed them in the chief scenes of the play.' But even if there was such a troupe in fact, it is doubtful if Utamaro needed their inspiration to design the set with women impersonating men, for it was quite in line with his normal policy, as shown in the *Silk-worm* series, the triptychs depicting the making of a colour-print, and so on.

The courtesans and geisha did, it is true, impersonate men in the famous *Niwaka* festival. The *Niwaka* culminated in a procession of these girls

81. *Seiōbō, the Fairy Queen of Chinese legend.*
From the series *Eight Charming Sages*. About 1795–7.

82. From the series *Brother and sister pictures.*
(An analogue of Yama-uba and Kintoki.) About 1796.

burlesqueing the cortège of the Korean ambassador, and many prints both of Utamaro and other artists portray the preparations for the event and record the mock procession. One of the finest of Utamaro's is a heptaptych. The first four sheets are filled by a group of girls carrying various banners on which the names of certain houses in the Yoshiwara are advertised. In the fifth sheet we see the palanquin of the 'queen' of the carnival, a geisha representing the ambassador and borne on the shoulders of a dozen of her companions. Behind come the dignitaries on horseback. This heptaptych belongs to the early years, and the printing, with pretty transparent effects in the pointed hats of Korean style, and in the hangings of the palanquin, is of the highest order (Fig. 78).

Perhaps the most recherché of even Utamaro's subjects, in which he makes a parody of a parody, is to be found in the set entitled *Eight Views of Biwa*.

The *Eight Views of Biwa* were a Japanese version of a famous set of traditional views of classical Chinese painting with Lake Tung-T'ing as their setting, and so were, in a sense, adaptations or, in the Japanese phrase, 'brother-pictures' already. These *Eight Views*, their setting transported to the shores of Lake Ōmi, or Biwa, perhaps the next most famous natural feature of the country after Mount Fuji, were followed with the strictness of ritual in all representations of the subject, latitude being allowed only in the treatment. The subjects have poetic titles: *Evening Snow on Hira*; *Return of Sailing Boats to Yabase*; *Twilight in Seta*; *Night Rain on Karasaki*; *Descent of the Wild Geese in Katata*; *Evening Bell at Miidera*; *Autumn Moon at Ishiyama Temple*; and *Clear Weather after Storm at Awazu*.

Utamaro has moved still further from the source in Lake Tung T'ing, and linked each of the well-known views with the affairs of famous lovers, often with shades of meaning in the title that need an expert interpreter. One instance from this set must suffice—the one entitled *Evening Snow*, reproduced as Fig. 80.

Here, in a small circle at the top of the print, is a snow scene from the *Eight Views* and the two figures of the print also portray a scene of wintry sadness, Sankatsu weeping whilst her lover Hanshichi bends over her. The sub-title of this print is *Sankatsu Hanshichi no Bosetsu*, and Mr Ledoux[1] has pointed out the *double-entendre*: the word *bosetsu*, meaning 'evening snow' in the usual *Eight View* series, also means the 'fidelity of a mother' and refers, by inference, to the loyalty of Hanshichi's wife Sankatsu. The various shifts from the original source remind one of the parlour game in which, by a series of slight changes to a given word, each making an intelligible word simply by altering the position of the letters, we arrive at another word bearing no apparent connection with the original. The Japanese language lends itself freely to punning, and sometimes the Ukiyo-e artists' involutions amount almost to 'pictorial punning'.

Not even the Gods and Immortals escaped travesty. Indeed, not the Ukiyo-e artists alone but painters of other schools, too, made free with the 'Seven Gods of Good Fortune', their very appearance in a picture was a signal for freedom and merriment, and no one took them seriously.

Utamaro, like the others, depicted the Seven Gods and the Ship of Good Fortune a number of times, and in a triptych of 1805 entitled *Fūryū Kotakarabune* ('Elegant Children's Ship of Good Fortune'), signed 'First drawing of the New Year' (for which a propitious subject was always chosen), he parodied the Gods as children. The Ship of Good Fortune is a boat on wheels with the prow shaped like the bird of good omen, the Hō-ō bird. Five children are in the boat, and at the stern a mother is helping a juvenile Fukurokuju into the boat, whilst at the side, a midget Daikoku is being suckled by his mother before he takes his ride.

Yet, despite the levity with which these Gods and certain Buddhistic worthies like Daruma were treated, Utamaro has been taken to task by critics for his depiction in a lovely series of prints of the Eight Immortals of Chinese Legend impersonated by courtesans. This set, *Enchū Hassen*, or 'Eight Charming Sages', dates from the time of the *Twelve Hours of the Green Houses*, and has the same characteristically tall, elongated figures, though the actual drawing shows a certain Kanō-esque brush-line that subtly adds to the travesty, such subjects being, of course, normally the prerogative of the aristocratic school.

One of this set is *A Beauty of the Day as Seiōbō* (Fig. 81). Seiōbō, the Chinese Fairy Queen, was able, by virtue of her peaches, to confer everlasting life upon mortals. Utamaro depicted her in the pose traditional to her in many Chinese and Kanō paintings that exist. She is the central figure, standing in her lovely finery beside a tall incense burner, whilst her attendant *kamuro* holds a dish of the 'peaches of longevity'. But Fenollosa[1] worked himself up into a fine indignation on this very print, using it to bring home charges of decadence and vulgarity, though surely he chose his ground badly. For even he cannot begrudge a certain 'extra-ordinary cleverness' to the drawing—'a force so striking and original that some persons have idealised it almost into a passion . . . The calligraphic pen strokes, as in the thin sash and the lower part of the drapery, sweep across the page like zig-zag flashes of lightning. . . . It is the genius of the twilight'. In the face of such words, the terms 'decadence' and 'vulgarity' seem singularly inappropriate.

[1]Ledoux, Louis V., *Japanese Prints Bunchō to Utamaro in the Collection of Louis V. Ledoux*.

[1]*An Outline History of Ukiyo-ye*. Tokyo, 1901.

XV. *The Niwaka Carnival, from the Annals of the Green Houses.* 1804.

XVI. *Geisha and attendant*. Brush painting. 1797–1800.
Haifa, Israel, Tikotin Museum of Japanese Art.

CHAPTER SEVENTEEN

UTAMARO'S BRUSH PAINTINGS

THE COLOUR-PRINT was, if not the 'poor man's painting', at least a substitute for one in the households of those people who could not ordinarily afford the luxury of the true brush painting. But many of the Ukiyo-e print-designers were primarily painters, and when amongst their clientèle they found a patron, they turned gladly to the task which gave them an opportunity to practise their true *métier*, and to vie with the members of the more exalted schools. On such occasions they were put on their mettle, invariably undertook such work with a seriousness often lacking in their designing for the print publishers: and men like Shunshō, Koryūsai and Eishi produced paintings that even the *cognoscenti* of Japan, unwilling though they are to accept the prints of those men as of any artistic consequence, are prepared to admit to a place, if not a high one, in company with the paintings of the masters of the Kanō, Chinese and other native aristocratic schools.

For this reason, if for no other, we in the West know far less of Ukiyo-e paintings than of prints, the finest having remained in Japanese hands since they were executed, only a few being available for inspection in European museums, though America has two very representative collections. But of Utamaro's brush paintings, not a single authentic example exists in our public collections, and our knowledge of his work in this medium, unless one is fortunate enough to be able to travel widely, is perforce limited to that acquired from reproductions. From the small number of these, however, it is clear that there are very few extant paintings. Anderson did not mention any, and Morrison spoke of his ability as a painter mainly by implication from his skill as a print-designer. De Goncourt in his monograph was able to mention only six. Neither of the two great exhibitions of Utamaro's works, in Paris in 1912, and in Tokyo in 1926, included a single painting by the master. It seems reasonable to conclude that his work as print-designer and book-illustrator precluded any great output of paintings. Unlike Hokusai's paintings, which loom large in any consideration of his powers, Utamaro's fall into a relatively unimportant place beside his prints, and his stature as an artist would not greatly be diminished if they were left out of account altogether.

It is noticeable, more with Utamaro probably than with other Ukiyo-e artists, that his paintings

83. *Ladies on a terrace by the sea*. Brush painting. About 1788–90. Washington, Freer Gallery of Art.

84. *Oiran and attendant*. Brush painting.
About 1787.
Boston, Mass., Museum of Fine Arts.

were executed with far more deference to orthodoxy than was felt necessary when drawing for the popular broadsheets. There is less playfulness, less experimentation, none of the daring in composition which repeatedly astounds us in the prints. They closely followed, in fact, the true Ukiyo-e style in the matter of technique, little deviating from the methods of the early masters, Moronobu, Chōshun, Sukenobu for example, so that Utamaro's paintings have a recognizable kinship with those of Moronobu, close to the very fount of Ukiyo-e, notwithstanding the enormous distance between his colour-prints and the broadsheets of the first Ukiyo-e master. Utamaro's paintings partake of the character general to Ukiyo-e painting—a greater realism than the Kanō masters were prepared to concede, bright opaque colours, and a delight in the detailed patterns of dresses, fine clear-cut bounding lines and a smooth finish; and for subject, the 'Floating World', the Yoshiwara and the tea-house. As a painter, he would of course have lacked the influence of a publisher, a Tsutajū, for instance, brimming over with ideas and projects, who might have prompted him to make innovations as daring in the *kakemono* as he made in the broadsheet. Whatever the reasons, he appears to have forfeited a great deal of his individuality in the brush medium, and no paintings are known that can vie with the finest of the prints.

As is to be expected, few paintings have survived of the earliest years, but during the period 1788–90, when he was giving evidence of his strength in such outstanding works as the *Insect Book* and other albums, and designing prints like the Enoshima triptych (Fig. 31), Utamaro executed a series of three unusually large paintings on the theme of *Setsu Gekka* ('*Snow, Moon and Flowers*') from which his ability at that time can be judged. It has been stated, though on what native authority I have not been able to learn, that this set of *kakemono* was painted for one Yoshino Zeneimon, who is credited with being Utamaro's first patron. However that may be, the three paintings still exist, one of them in two versions,[1] and two are reproduced here (Figs. 83, 86).

[1]The 'Moon' subject (Fig. 83). Mr. Harold P. Stern, in an interesting paper read before the Far Eastern Association, 30 March 1955, makes a convincing case for the authenticity of the Freer painting. The other is reproduced in *Ukiyo-e Taika Shusei*, 1931, but its present whereabouts is not known. The 'Snow' painting is in a Japanese collection.

In neither of the pictures reproduced has Utamaro successfully co-ordinated the large number of
figures and the wide extent of the scene: in the
Flower scene, there is an unpleasant overcrowding;
in the *Moon*, there are empty spaces that are
simply blank and of no significance in the composition. Both rely to a great extent on a sort of
Ukiyo-e 'perspective', a half-understood application
of the European system, quite inimical to the true
Japanese method of indicating spatial relation-
ships. In short, both pictures are better seen in
section than as a whole, and single figures have
much of the charm of the girls of the prints. The
three paintings represent an enormous endeavour
on the part of the artist, and should no doubt be
looked upon as 'diploma' works, with just the sort
of failings to be expected from such an ambitious
over-straining of his powers.

The types depicted are essentially Kiyonaga-
esque, the tall but well-proportioned girls with
rounded faces of sweet expression are unmistakable, and, in fact, the *Moon* picture has a setting
very similar to that of one of Kiyonaga's most
famous diptychs *A Terrace by the Sea*, in which a
company of courtesans and a young man are
amusing themselves in a room that, like the one in
Utamaro's picture, gives upon the sea-shore.

But these large paintings are exceptional. Generally the paintings are in the more normal *kakemono*
form, the tall upright oblong, and the subject of
most is usually a single courtesan or perhaps two,
with an attendant *kamuro*, or else a male servant,
carrying an umbrella, though some depict a mother
and child.[1]

One of the earliest, of the same date as the
Setsugekka in fact, is in the Museum of Fine Arts,
Boston (Fig. 85). This far simpler work is much
more satisfying as a work of art than those crowded
panoramas, and shows to perfection the quietism
that constitutes one of the pleasures of this stock
type of Ukiyo-e *bijin-ga*. The sure brush describes a
series of suave flowing curves which fall and eddy
with the fluidity of a heavy oil. The colour is solid
and definite and the artist makes great play of the
patterns of the dresses.

The *Geisha and Attendant* (Plate XVI) is a painting of the artist's maturity, and is, in every way, a

85. *Girl with a wasps' nest.* Brush painting.
About 1800. Boston, Mass., Museum of Fine Arts.

[1] Reproductions of several of these are to be found in *Ukiyo-e Taika Shusei*,
1931, and Yoshida, *Utamaro Zenshū*, 1941.

86. *The fête of flowers in the Yoshiwara*. Brush painting. About 1788–90. Formerly Mme Berès collection.

bolder piece of work than the last, some ten years earlier. The figures are more monumental and make a stronger arabesque. The line is freer and more eventful. Perhaps in this painting, Utamaro came nearer than in most to achieving an éclat equal to that of the prints: yet a glance at the reproductions of the great prints of this period (Chapter XV) shows at once the limitations more or less enforced on the painter by the brush medium and the *kakemono* format: the unusual *mise-en-page*, the unorthodox angle of sighting the figures, the novelty of cutting into a group with the boundary line of the print and of giving some figures full length, others three-quarters, others head and shoulders only— all these devices and varying ploys have been neglected in the paintings, with great loss of effectiveness.

Apart from the *Kakemono*, a few sketches are

known, some like the *Girl with a Wasps' Nest* (Fig. 85) and two paintings reproduced in *Taika Shūsei*, made without any apparent object in view, others evidently preparatory for colour-prints. The latter are naturally extremely uncommon, since in Utamaro's day it seems generally to have been the custom, though not universally, to paste the artist's design on to the block, and only in rare instances were copies made of the artist's original for the use of the block-cutter (a practice that seems to have increased in later years judging by the number of Hokusai's drawings that have been preserved). In any case, such drawings were considered of no account: they merely set in train the chain of processes resulting in the end-product, the colour-print. They were considered to have no intrinsic value of their own, and were only preserved by chance (Fig. 2).

CHAPTER EIGHTEEN

THE YAMA-UBA AND KINTOKI SERIES AND THE 'MOTHER AND CHILD' PRINTS

THE STORY OF Kintoki 'the golden boy' is one of the favourite legends of Japan. Yorimitsu, one of the great warrior heroes of the Middle Ages, out hunting one day, and pushing into the inner recesses of the mountain called Ashigara in Sagami province, came upon a child with the physique of an infant Hercules, and a skin that was brick-red, engaged in playing with a bear cub. At Yorimitsu's bidding the boy went in search of his mother. She was a tall woman of wild appearance, with long black hair falling about her shoulders, clad only in a

87. *Kintoki covering Yama-Uba's face with a mask of O-Kame, the goddess of Mirth or Folly.* 1796–9.

garment of leaves, although she spoke the language of the Court. This was Yama-Uba, the 'Mountain Mother', who recounted how after the boy's father, a great general of the Minamoto clan, had been killed in a battle with the Taira, she had brought up Kintoki with the intention of making a hero of him.

Yorimitsu requested that Kintoki be put in his care, and Yama-Uba gave way. The boy grew up, took the name of Sakata-no-Kintoki, from the province granted him by Yorimitsu, and became one of Yorimitsu's principal officers. In this capacity, he was the hero of a number of legends, perhaps the best known being the worsting of a notorious brigand called Shūten-dōji, and the expedition to discover and kill a gigantic spider that had wounded Yorimitsu, and all recount feats of bravery and strength of Kintoki that are as well-known to the Japanese as to us the Twelve Labours of Hercules.

He is a particularly popular subject with the Ukiyo-e print-designers, especially as a young boy. He is invariably depicted as an infant with chubby limbs of even brick-red colour, accompanied by an immense axe which he carries as an emblem of his strength and courage. In a large group of prints designed at the end of the century, Utamaro concentrated on the relationship between this lusty, mischievous boy and his mother, whom he depicts as a woman of the same elemental nature as the strange Awabi-fishers of the famous triptych.

He was obviously strongly attracted by the potentialities of this strange companionship, imbues the lady of the court, who has retired to the wilderness, with a mysterious, disturbing character, brooding sombrely over her charge at one moment, laughingly teasing him the next, a veritable spirit of the mountains; and depicts with delicious humour the impotent annoyance of the child, who, whilst conscious of his supernatural gifts, is treated by his mother as an ordinary baby, fondled and nursed and made to suffer all the little indignities necessary in the cause of hygiene or Japanese custom. Usually, you are made to sense a sort of truculence in his attitude, he resents Yama-Uba's mothering and

88. *Yama-Uba and Kintoki.* 1796–9.

mocks her tenderness, though now and again he is a true baby with a real affection for his guardian.

Only a few of these prints are given titles: the deep red colour of the boy, the long hair of the woman falling about her shoulders, identified the subject at once. The prints fall into two categories, one in which the pair are depicted full length, the other where only the head and shoulders of Yama-Uba are given, a type reminiscent of the *Large Heads* being produced at the same period.

Among those of the former type, Yama-Uba is shown holding an enormous mirror whilst Kintoki, seated on her lap, is pulling a ferocious face as she looks in it; or Yama-Uba is seated wearing a robe

89. *Yama-Uba and Kintoki.* 1796–9.

patterned with chrysanthemums, as Kintoki dresses her hair, he standing on the stump of a felled tree to reach her head, with a face set in belligerent distaste for the job; or he bestrides Yama-Uba's back as, nude to the waist, she bends forward to comb her immensely long hair; or she is shaving the crown of the boy's head (in keeping with the custom with Japanese children until the age of four or five),

Kintoki holding his axe under his chin, instead of the usual barber's board, to catch the clippings; or under a gnarled old tree, Yama-Uba 'holds him out' while he drowsily strokes her chin, holding his huge axe by the handle. We are shown Kintoki at Yama-Uba's breast (children continued to be fed by their mothers far longer than is common here), his mischievous eyes roving about him as he distractedly bends to his task (Fig. 88); and in the lovely print of larger dimensions than usual known as *The Chestnut* (Fig. 90), Yama-Uba is making game of him, tantalizingly holding the chestnut high out of his reach, and he in a tantrum is storming at her, reaching up, one foot off the ground, and clutching at her waist.

The 'close-ups' are remarkable for the expressiveness of the faces, and for the intense emotion expressed in certain of the prints, especially the one in which they passionately kiss. In another, however, the fond mother embraces Kintoki with both arms around his neck, but he, holding her wrists, is truculently opposing her show of affection. In others, Yama-Uba is cleaning his ear with a point stick, under which treatment he closes one eye and twists his mouth in stoically-endured pain; or she is smoking, and Kintoki forces her head up as she blows out smoke; or she has tied his hands with a kite string and laughs openly at his rage; or she holds him high in her arms and he with glee reaches down for the whistle she holds between her lips.

All told, these prints form a remarkable group, standing quite outside the main body of Utamaro's prints, just as the *Awabi Fishers* triptych does. Yama-Uba is a woman apart, owing none of her attraction to exquisite finery, for she is usually in the simplest garment with little or no decoration, and with her unkempt hair and wild aspect, the very antithesis of the elegant painted women of the town: but in her Utamaro has portrayed a deep and elemental nature, capable of intense feeling. It has been suggested that even these seemingly innocent prints had a covertly erotic significance.

The special distinction of the *Kintoki* prints becomes at once apparent if they are compared with other prints having a 'Mother and Child' subject, several series of which were published about the same time. In these, the mother is invariably the same beautifully robed creature we are familiar with, her milieu the pretty apartments of an Edo villa, the children the most natural and unheroic of offspring, and the scenes set in an atmosphere of urbane domesticity that is far removed from the world of fantasy in which Yama-Uba and Kintoki have their being.

There is, in fact, a set entitled *E-kyō-dai* ('*Brother and Sister pictures*') which links the world of heroic legend with familiar Edo. At the top of each print there is a small inset drawing recording some well-known incident from one of the legends: in the main body of the print, the scene is vaguely paralleled by a domestic scene. In the inset of one, Kintoki is wrestling with a bear-cub with Yama-Uba watching: below, a woman with long hair that streams down to the floor, and so reminding us of Yama-Uba, watches her child playing with a cat. The drawing of the mother and child is superb and I would be inclined to place this print rather earlier than most of the *Kintoki* series, say about 1796. Another print in this set parodies the story of Inohayata despatching the fiend Nue, Yorimasa, who had wounded him with an arrow; standing by with a huge burning brand. In the main body of the print, a young lad, with top of head shaved, has captured a rat under a box, which he holds above it with ferocious determination, his mother, a tall figure in a lovely purple over-garment, standing by with lighted taper in her upraised hand.

Of the other prints of *Mother and Child* there are dozens, and in none of his many works does Utamaro give greater evidence of his geniality, his quiet humour; and if we begin to notice a falling-off in the composition and draughtsmanship in some, there are still many grand designs among them.

Possibly the best known of this type is the often reproduced print of a young mother seated before a mirror on a lacquer stand and suckling her baby, the back of whose pathetically bald little head we see reflected in the mirror. This is a beautiful design —the whole form and attitude of the mother seems to envelop and protect the child. Another depicts a mother holding her darling whilst father shaves his head with a razor, and there is a world of expressiveness in the resignation of the baby to his fate, and the open-mouthed anxiety of the mother. In the set *Fūzoku Bijin Tokei* ('*The Twelve Hours Represented by Women*') at the Hour of the Rat a young mother is aroused from her sleep and is seen emerging from the inevitable mosquito net, holding her plump baby beneath the thighs for the purpose usually associated with small-hour disturbances, whilst he drowsily rubs his eyes and contorts himself in a paroxysm of yawning.

We are shown mother and child, or both parents and child, in an immense variety of occupations. One of the loveliest and earliest sets is entitled *Ukiyo nanatsu me awase* ('*Seven eyes watching together*'). In one print a little boy held in his mother's arms reaches down to touch a white rabbit that is crouching on the husband's shoulder, the 'seven eyes' being those of the three human beings, and the one eye that is visible of the rabbit. Another from this set, of which there are a number, each with a tacitly posed problem 'find the seven eyes', shows a seated girl allowing a white mouse to run up her bared arm for the amusement of a little boy held by the mother in her arm. A print with a similar playful idea behind it is called *Kokei Sanshō* ('*The Three Laughers*'). Here a mother with a child carried pick-a-back bends over a stone trough of water so that both their faces are mirrored in the water. A dog, the third laugher, lifts his paw and seems to beg to be allowed to see *his* face in the water.

The mirror motif, a favourite one with Utamaro throughout his life, is again used in one of the later sets having a mother and child for subject, that entitled *Futaba gusa nana Kōmachi* ('*Seven Komachi of Two-leaved Grass*'), which is a wonderfully involved example of the kind of analogue already discussed in Chapter XVI. The 'two-leaved grass' is an allusion to the intimate relationship between mother and child. Laurence Binyon[1] aptly refers to Shakespeare's 'a lovely union: two berries on one bough'. The traditional scene from the life of Komachi parodied by the mother and child who bend over a basin of water to see their reflected images is known as *Komachi of the Parrot*. The emperor Yosei sent a poem to the poetess, which she returned with only one character altered, a kind of 'echo-poem' that was named after the parrot. In this print, the reflection of the two faces, only subtly altered by the faint tone of the water in the bowl, stands for the 'echo-poem' of the poetess — an intricate explanation for a little print that needs no literary allusion to add to its charm.

Finally, there is what is perhaps the best known of these sets, the *Fūryū kodakara awase* ('*Elegant set of Darling Children*'), of which the one of the little boy upsetting a goldfish bowl whilst the mother lies asleep, leaning on her workbox, is perhaps my favourite, the quiet methodical air with which the little 'darling' is holding down the edge of the bowl to allow the water to gush over the floor being a wonderful touch (Fig. 92).

But I can only mention a tithe—there exist scores of equally pleasant prints with similar subjects that show Utamaro's invention at its best, with bright

[1]The British Museum Catalogue.

90. *The Chestnut: Yama-Uba and Kintoki.* 1796–9.

colour schemes that are all of a piece with the playful mood in which they were designed. And all these were composed at a time of life when Fenollosa and others condemn him for degeneracy, for enfeeblement from immorality, although no active artist, save possibly Hokusai, then slowly coming to the fore, could have held a candle to him for fecundity, powers of invention, geniality, and mature easy draughtsmanship.

91. *Mother and child looking at their reflections in a water-trough,*
from *Eight Views of the Mirror of Courtesans.* 1797–8.

風流子寶合

哥麿筆

92. *Child upsetting a goldfish bowl*, from a set entitled *Elegant Set of Darling Children*.
About 1800.

CHAPTER NINETEEN

THE 'ANNALS OF THE GREEN HOUSES' · PORTRAITS OF UTAMARO

APART FROM a few *kibyōshi* and erotic books, no dated books illustrated by Utamaro appeared between 1791 and 1800, though during these years he contributed single prints to a few albums (the *Otoko Tōka* of 1798 has already been referred to), and certain of the undated erotica undoubtedly belong to this period. In 1801, however, appeared the two little volumes entitled *Shiki no hana* ('*Flowers of the Four Seasons*', with the meaning, as ever, of 'Flowers of the Yoshiwara throughout the Year'). The first volume opens with a frontispiece of yellow blossoms, and thereafter follow pages of lovely girls in the dresses of spring and summertime, pursuing the round of their leisure, in the open air for the most part. We see them playing at battledore, collecting herbs, boarding a pleasure boat, crowding across the Ryōgoku Bridge, and, as night falls, fixing the mosquito nets. This print alone (Fig. 93) is eloquent of the change in Utamaro's art since the fine *Sojourners at an Inn* triptych of the mid-nineties, for although pleasantly composed and tastefully coloured, it lacks the inspired draughtsmanship, the refined harmony of tones and the tender spirit that make the earlier work so outstanding a masterpiece.

In the second volume, a frontispiece of chrysanthemums betokens the autumnal and winter scenes that are to follow. Girls are seen on the verandah on

93. *Fixing the mosquito-net: the Thunderstorm*, from *Flowers of the Four Seasons*. 1801.

a moonlight night or on an outing to view the chrysanthemums in flower; in one print, a girl is sitting in a litter beside a stream beneath autumnal maples; in another an interior is shown, with girls seeking warmth beneath the coverlet called a *futon*, on which a cat has ensconced himself; but the loveliest design is of two girls caught in a sudden squall with umbrellas raised against the driving rain (Fig. 94).

All told, whatever its shortcomings compared with earlier and grander works, *Shiki no hana* is a charming little book, which from another artist would have been hailed with far greater acclaim: but it has been persistently belittled because of more splendid precursors.

The last dated book illustrated by Utamaro, and the one known most widely, the *Seirō Ehon Nenjū Gyōji* ('*Annals of the Green Houses*') appeared in 1804. To the able text of Jippensha Ikku, Utamaro added a series of prints which only one with the long experience of the affairs of the Yoshiwara could have produced. In the colophon of the book itself,

collaboration is acknowledged with three of his pupils, Kikumaro, Hidemaro and Takemaro, whose own work is normally without any great distinction. Just what the collaboration implied, whether these assistants were allowed to prepare designs of their own or, more likely, simply filled in the details of sketches supplied by the master, there is no means of telling, but it raises in one's mind the question of how much of Utamaro's late work was 'studio work' of this kind, instigated and signed by him, but in reality largely the work of pupils. At any rate, this book abounds in felicities that, but for the acknowledged help of pupils, we would at once have thought of as Utamaro's own.

The book was one of the first to arouse the curiosity of the West in Utamaro's work, and de Goncourt evidently attached great importance to it, partly because of the vivid pictures it gives of that curious world-within-a-world, the Yoshiwara. For the period, there is an unusual care in the engraving and printing. A few copies exist printed from the key-blocks only, in black ink, and de

94. *A sudden squall: courtesan and attendant,* from *Flowers of the Four Seasons.* 1801.

95. *In the cage*, from the *Annals of the Green Houses*. 1804.

Goncourt's own copy of this edition is now in the British Museum.

Two or three of the prints are of special interest. In one (Fig. 95), Utamaro has depicted a group of courtesans in the street-side trellis cages where they sat under the eyes of the passers-by for hours on end, idling the time away in a variety of ways, smoking, writing letters, or gossiping. One is making an assignation with a man who has placed his head close to the bars.

This display of wares in the open market brings home to us more forcibly than any other scene the true nature of the occupation of these women, so easily forgotten in the artist's absorption with the colourful pageantry of their ceremonial, but Ikku, the writer of the text, is harrowed by no such distracting thoughts. He takes the occasion to enlarge, somewhat in the manner of Utamaro the Physiognomist, on the characters of the young ladies. 'She who is engrossed in reading a book,' he writes, 'taking no notice of the teasing amongst the others, is the one who would entertain you most pleasantly once you have become intimate with her. She who

now and then whispers to her neighbours, hides her face to stifle her laughter and looks at a man square in the face, is capable of throwing you over with some surprising trick. She who has her hands thrust deeply down within her dress and her chin tucked into her neck, looking long into space, she hides an aching heart. She won't be very amusing the first times, but the day you have won her heart she won't let you go free any more. She who teases, exchanges pleasantries, laughs with the under-mistress and turns abruptly to hear the words of a passer-by is a very capricious creature. If you are to her taste, very soon you'll be her darling. She who is writing several letters is the woman who wants a clientèle. To win her heart would be difficult, but if you are old, unlovable and ugly, you will make a very powerful impression on her—if you have money. She who, still a youngster, spends her time playing, is still an innocent—with her you could do much as you pleased.'

There is a great deal of humour in the print entitled *The first meeting: the first night*, showing four men seated in an elegant reception room

96. *Utamaro painting a Hō-ō bird in one of the Green Houses*, from the *Annals of the Green Houses*. 1804.

lighted by tapers in tall holders, awaiting the occasion to make the first overtures, 'If you do not come to an agreement the first time and you are patient,' says Ikku, 'on the second visit you can pursue the formalities with redoubled vigour.'

But perhaps the most intimate and revealing picture is that of *The Morning After*. In this we are shown the courtesans and attendants busying themselves in tidying up their rooms, kindling the charcoal fire, fetching water in a bowl, preparing tea, whilst the man sits apart—a masterly touch this—a stranger among intimates, one leg doubled under him as he sits on the window seat, pensively cleaning his teeth and looking out, rather morosely one suspects, on roof-tops and branches white with snow (Fig. 97).

The last print in the second volume is a self-portrait of the artist at work on a giant painting of a Hō-ō bird on a sliding screen in one of the Green Houses (Fig. 96). Utamaro was a man past fifty at the time this book was published, and one can place no reliance on this drawing as a portrait, but

it is typical that he should have depicted himself in the act of painting. In a much earlier print (Fig. 99), one of a series of the *Four Accomplishments*, he had portrayed himself as the personification of Painting: it was in keeping with the idealization of his features that he should have represented himself always in the guise of a painter rather than a designer of prints.

Perhaps in this place might be mentioned the disputed portrait of Utamaro by Eishi in the British Museum (Fig. 98). When Arthur Morrison first described and reproduced it,[1] it was accepted without demur as a memorial portrait of Utamaro, painted, as was customary, after his death, but by one who knew his lineaments sufficiently well to reproduce a living likeness—it was one of the rare exceptions to the general practice of idealization. Among prints that are of this type, probably the best known are Kunisada's portrait of Hiroshige, and Toyokuni's of Eijudō, the publisher.

[1] *Ostasiatische Zeitschrift*, 1912.

97. *The Morning After*, from the *Annals of the Green Houses*. 1804.

The portrait, too, seemed to accord with the generally held view of a life of dissipation. In Eishi's portrait, whilst I would not go so far as to say that he appears 'fat, flabby, bent and prematurely aged', or as a 'corpulent man prematurely aged with flaccid cheeks, baggy eyes, bent back and with a bloated and repellent aspect' as some have described him, he certainly does present a rather repulsive countenance that might easily be that of an elderly roué. But Eishi had carefully signed the portrait *Utamaro no zō Chōbunsai Eishi gyōnen roku-jū sai hitsu* ('*Portrait of Utamaro painted by Chōbunsai Eishi in the sixtieth year of his age*') and when some thirty years ago the date of Eishi's birth was for the first time established, it proved that the painting had been executed in 1815, nine years after Utamaro's death, and thus much later than one would normally have expected a memorial portrait to have been painted.

This discrepancy in date led Binyon and Sexton to conclude that the painting must therefore have been a portrait of Utamaro's follower who appropriated his name after 1806, Baigadō Utamaro,

the man responsible for many of the late prints bearing the signature 'Utamaro'. Binyon and Sexton also stated that another painting by Eishi exists 'similarly signed, but without the age, which depicts a man of middle age, of serious demeanour, intelligent and somewhat ascetic-looking, grasping in his left hand a rosary; undoubtedly a memorial portrait of the great master Utamaro I, painted just after his death on October 31st, 1806'. This second portrait can no longer be traced, but it is reproduced from an old photograph in *Ukiyo-e*, No. 50, 1966, p. 94.

In the British Museum portrait, the sitter wears a black outer garment on which appears the three-leaf *mon* (crest) of Utamaro, and beneath, he has on a blue red-edged dress. He is seated, pipe in hand, on a cushion decorated with sprigs of pinks.

Whilst admitting the counter-evidence of the date, and of the other portrait by Eishi presenting so different a person, there are two or three reasons why it is difficult to reject the British Museum Eishi as a genuine portrait of Utamaro. For one thing, there is no record of any association of Eishi with the second Utamaro, who was, in any case, an insignificant artist that a painter of Eishi's eminence was hardly likely to commemorate. Furthermore, there is evidence that the second Utamaro was still alive in 1817, and the need for a memorial portrait could not have arisen in 1815. Then again, whenever the Japanese artist did resort to actual portraiture, he obtained his effect, owing to the oriental method of painting without chiaroscuro, by emphasizing the *lines* of the features, so producing what often seems to us to be near-caricature. The rather flabby features and the fleering lips of the portrait need not imply that the sitter was 'a worn-out roué' if that is one of the objections which led Binyon and Sexton, great protagonists of Utamaro, to reject it. At fifty-three, after a sedentary life such as Utamaro's constant industry must have imposed, the baggy eyes and flaccid cheeks might just as well have been the result of unceasing effort as of dissipation. I would find it easier to accept this as a portrait of Utamaro than the other, which portrays a man 'of serious demeanour, intelligent and somewhat ascetic-looking'.

98. *Portrait of Utamaro*. Brush-painting by Eishi. 1815. London, British Museum.

99. *Utamaro personifying Painting*. 1790–1.

CHAPTER TWENTY

UTAMARO'S LAST YEARS

OF THE YEARS 1800 to 1806, the least important from the aspect of Utamaro's art, we have the greatest number of reasonably authentic facts concerning his life, not, it is true, of much value in indicating the type of man he really was, but bringing a little definition to a figure that hitherto is but shadowy. Moreover, the growing practice of stamping prints with the date-seal of the year of issue enables us to date some of the prints of this last period with certainty.

Acknowledged leader of the Ukiyo-e school, he now had only one serious rival, not Hokusai who, still a young man, was feeling his way, but Toyokuni, an artist emanating from the Utagawa sub-school. Toyokuni was a man of every gift except originality; eclectic and plagiaristic, there was something slightly coarse and unrefined in his successive versions of Kiyonaga, Shunshō, Shunchō, Sharaku, Eishi and Utamaro, from all of whom he borrowed without shame. He was exceptionally prolific, even among the colour-print artists, and after 1800 obviously appealed to the now less cultured taste of the Edo men and women, especially with his shoddy actor-prints which he turned out by the hundred.

Echoes of the rivalry between these two dominating artists have come down to us. A traveller in the northern parts of Japan in these years, a man who was apparently a collector of prints, has left it on record that in all the provinces of Japan, Utamaro was considered the greatest master of the land, whilst Toyokuni was much less known. Utamaro's prints were exported to China and bought by the Dutch at Nagasaki. The description of certain prints in the early nineteenth-century inventory of property belonging to a family called Titsingh in Amsterdam, one of whose members had been head of the Dutch trading centre at Nagasaki in the eighties, tallies with certain types of Utamaro's prints, and makes it almost certain that his prints reached Europe during his lifetime, though surprisingly enough they appear to have given rise to little curiosity at the time concerning this branch of the art of the East.

Hashirakake of a special size exist, rather broader than the normal, commissioned by the publisher Iwatoya Kisaburō both from Toyokuni and from Utamaro about 1800–2, whilst each was at the height of his popularity (Figs. 100, 101). The *hashirakake* was, as the name implies, a pillar-hanging print, usually about 27 inches by 4 to 5 inches, expressly designed to decorate the wooden pillars of the Japanese house, and mounted, as often as not, on rollers, like the paintings of the country. They represent a format quite foreign to any with which we are familiar. The long, narrow print was a supreme test of an artist's powers of composition, and Harunobu and Koryūsai, and, to a lesser extent, Eishi, Kiyonaga and Shunchō, excelled in contrivances that would fill naturally the exacting shape. Strangely enough, Utamaro was only occasionally attracted to the *hashirakake*, and his prints in this form are relatively few and mostly from the later periods of his life; though in a shape nearer the true *kakemono*, like these prints commissioned by Iwatoya, he did some splendid designs, notably the print known as *The Chestnut* (Fig. 90).

Comparison of the prints which Utamaro and Toyokuni designed for Iwatoya does not show any marked superiority in Utamaro's, and only proves how closely Toyokuni approached his contemporary when, as in this case, he was on his mettle. But some of Utamaro's are in his best vein, with touches reminiscent of the playfulness and charm of earlier years. In one (Fig. 100) a woman is standing and looking down at her little boy, who has placed his head under her diaphanous kimono, through which his face can be seen. In another a woman on a verandah, stooping over a stone cistern, lifts out a block of ice at the end of her dipper (Fig. 101)—a favourite motif for indicating the rigours of winter. A third shows a couple in a boat, fishing with rod and line under the piles of the Ryōgoku Bridge. The girl has just hooked a tiny fish which she grips with her left hand as it dangles at the end of her uplifted rod; the man is dipping his *sake*-cup in the river, and in opposition to all we are taught of the practice of Japanese painting, his reflection is

100. *Baby peering through its mother's Kimono.*
About 1803–4.

plainly indicated in the water. Whilst this departure—not by any means uncommon in Ukiyo-e prints—may indicate that Utamaro, too, like Hokusai and others, was flirting with European methods, the reflection was probably introduced into this print for the way in which it lengthened the figures out to fill the long panel and so give a sense of completeness to the design.

It may have been a desire to compete with Toyokuni on his own ground that led Utamaro in 1803 to design a theatrical print, breaking with his usual practice of eschewing the stage. It commemorates a play produced in 1803 in which the actors were Ichikawa Yaozō, who played the male part of Chōemon, and Iwai Kumesaburō, who played the female lead, O-Han. In the print Chōemon has just crossed a stream with O-Han upon his back, and an interesting inscription, which may easily have been directed obliquely at Toyokuni and his followers, who were now flooding the print shops with gaudily-coloured and carelessly-printed actor-prints, runs as follows:

'My picture of O-Han and Chōemon is not a mere unskilful imitation. Yaozō comes from a good-looking family and Kumesaburō is the actor of the day of woman's parts. Both have an elegant manner on the stage, and I fervently wish, by means of my humble brush, to spread the beauty of the actors of Edo throughout the country.'

Though by no means outstanding among Utamaro's prints, it shows a welcome restraint and care when placed beside any of Toyokuni's of the period.

Another fact for which we have the evidence of at least three nearly contemporary accounts, conflicting though they be in details, is the imprisonment of Utamaro in 1804 or 1805 (probably the latter), for offences against certain proscriptive laws.

The causes of Utamaro's imprisonment are dealt with exhaustively in Binyon and Sexton's *Japanese Colour Prints*, where the evidence of the contemporary writers who report the affair is sifted, and reproductions given of some of the rare prints that incurred the sentence (Fig. 105). The law contravened by these prints was that forbidding the identification, by name or crest, of men famous in history, or of particularly honourable memory. A triptych published in 1804 had as its subject the Taikō (that is, Hideyoshi, the great national hero of the sixteenth century) and his five wives pleasure-viewing at Rakutō, an event vouched for by history, which tells how Hideyoshi, relaxing from the great affairs of state, repaired to the temple gardens at Daigo, east of Kyōto, accompanied by his wife and four concubines. But the offence was not, as was earlier conjectured, an aspersion thus indirectly cast upon the morals of the Shōgun of the day, but simply that these personages were identified on the print by names (somewhat garbled) and *mon* or crests. For his part in the production of this print—one of the most uncharacteristic we have from his hand, feebly designed and repellent in colour—Utamaro was apparently censured. Early in the following year, however, appeared a series of single-sheets of his designing which depicted other scenes from the life of the Taikō, and these were not only of an order to ridicule the man of illustrious memory, but repeated the offence of naming. Accordingly, Utamaro was committed to prison, by one account for three days, and suffered the further ignominy of being forced to wear handcuffs upon his release for fifty days.

About this time there was evidently another wave of puritanic zeal in government circles, perhaps because a growing freedom among the lower orders required checking. Shunei and other Ukiyo-e artists paid the penalty for trifling with laws that seem only to have been rigorously enforced when one of the periodic 'purges' was decreed.

Whether the effect of Utamaro's punishment was to hasten, as has been suggested, an enfeeblement in his art and a premature end to his life, can hardly be determined now. A few typical works of the last five years dispel any idea that Utamaro was a spent force before the event, but there are few works that can reliably be dated after 1805.

One of the finest works of the period is the remarkable twelve-sheet print of silk-worm culture, *Jōshoku kaiko tewaza kusa*, designed as a continuous panorama. It was singularly appropriate that the Ukiyo-e artists should have given so many presentations of this subject, their broadsheets depending so largely upon the beauty of the patterned silks worn by the people. A number of conventions became established in these pictures of seri-culture; the labourers were always women, the mulberry leaf and the cocoons invariably far larger than they are in reality; and Utamaro was simply following tradition when he gave coolie tasks to elegant young

101. *The Frozen Dipper.*
About 1803–4.

102. From the series *Ten Forms of Feminine Physiognomy*. About 1802.

103. From the series *Ten Forms of Feminine Physiogmony*. About 1802.

104. *Silk worms being fed with mulberry leaves*. From the twelve-sheet print of Silk-worm Culture. About 1802.

ladies in mock-working clothes that, like those of the shepherdesses in our own 'pastorals', suggest the boudoir rather than the field. The first and much superior edition of this print is printed in an unusual and very lively colour scheme of violet, blue, green, yellow and grey, and there is such fertility of invention in the composition, so pleasant an air throughout, that one would hesitate to say, from the evidence of this print of about 1802, that Utamaro's art was in a decline (Fig. 104).

But in two or three other sets published about this time, Utamaro tried to repeat successes of earlier years, and it is then, with both works before us, that we can best judge of the fall in power. In one set, even the title is identical—*Fūjin Sō Gaku Jittai* ('*Ten Forms of Feminine Physiognomy*')—there is a similar triple-panelled cartouche giving title, character of the woman portrayed and his signature—Kansō Utamaro again, 'Utamaro the Physiognomist': mica, too, is used in some as background.

真柴久吉

哥麿筆

105. One of the prints responsible for Utamaro's imprisonment. The inscription 'Mashiba Hisayoshi' only faintly
disguises Hashiba Hideyoshi, and shows the great general fondling his favourite page. About 1805.

One depicts a girl whose wrap has fallen from her shoulders as she combs her long hair—'She behaves correctly', says the caption. 'She is capable of great passion, but she will not easily surrender to it.' (Fig. 102). Another is of a girl with a lantern that casts its beam upwards, illuminating her face. Her 'character', reading like a motto from a Christmas cracker, is 'She is charming and faithful, and men are foolish over her.' A third, 'She who has this sort of countenance is very gentle in her nature and works hard, often harder than is known' is appropriately shown turning the handle of a stone-mill (Fig. 103). But the connection between the character inscribed on the print and the girl portrayed, not always apparent to us even in the earlier series of 1791–2, has disappeared completely, the labels are applied to girls quite pleasantly drawn but lacking, above all, in character. And that Utamaro's sense of design was faltering can be seen by comparing reproductions from the earlier with the later sets.

106. *Rikomono, 'The Clever Person',*
reading Ehon Taiko-ki, a history of Taikō Hideyoshi.
From the set *Through the Parents' Moralizing Spectacles.*
1803-4.

The insistence on 'character' amounts almost to moralizing in a well-known set entitled *Kyōkun oya no megane* ('*Through the Parents' Moralizing Spectacles*'), on each print of which the title is given inside the red frame of a pair of spectacles. Each depicts a half-length figure of a girl and has a lengthy text giving her 'character'. A plump woman making sheep's eyes as she holds a fan behind her head is condemned as a 'Lewd Person', another feasting on crab and with a European-shaped wine glass in her hand is the 'Spoiled Child' of whom the inscription says, among other edifying remarks, 'This kind of girl has never been well-trained. Nothing worse can be said about them.' It is interesting to observe in another that the book a girl is reading as she reclines with her neck on her pillow is none other than a volume of *Ehon Taikō-ki*, illustrated by an Osaka artist, Gyokusan, which, published during the years 1797–1802, be-

came immediately popular, and resulted indirectly in the colour-prints by Utamaro and Shunei that led to their imprisonment. The book was banned in 1804. (Fig. 106).

A triptych entitled *A Party of Women and Children in the Grounds of a Temple* has a seal date corresponding to the year 1805–6, and must be one of the last prints designed by Utamaro (Fig. 107). Compared with earlier atmospheric *plein air* pictures, there is a lack of grace in the figures, a dull perfunctoriness in the drawing of the trees and other landscape features, and no understandable relationship between the temple visitors and the setting. The loss of naturalness in the disposition of figures and their integration with their surroundings is all too apparent when this late print is placed alongside that illustrated in Fig. 19, designed some twenty years earlier.

Another inevitable comparison is suggested by the late triptych of Seven Ri Beach, with a party of women on the way to the isle of Enoshima and the Shrine of Benten (one of the Seven Gods of Good Fortune). The pleasure-goers and pilgrims on the beach, the little girl who has picked up a shell and is showing it to her parents, all the happenings and the surroundings recall the former prints, but the drawing is hurried, the engraving and printing slovenly and lacking all those splendours of colour and exquisite dress pattern that make the earlier prints of Enoshima beach so enchanting.

But not all the triptychs of these years are cause for regret. From the immense number of three-sheet prints being produced at the time it is still possible to pick a handful that are capable of surprising us by their originality, their verve, the flair for composition that was the last of Utamaro's gifts to desert him.

There is, for example, the *Princess descending from her carriage*, a colourful print that crosses the border of fantasy into a fairyland world in which a princess alights from a carriage fit for travel along no ordinary highway, with panels of purple floral pattern and framework lacquered black. In another we are back among the ordinary Edo folk we have come to know so well, seeking shelter from a sudden summer storm. The rain lashes down in diagonal rods, and the thunder roars: one girl claps her hands to her ears and a little tot wails, begging to be picked up by its mother, already holding one child on her arm. A girl in the strangely shaped straw hat of summertime ties her girdle, loosened in

107. *A Party of Women and Children in the Grounds of a Temple.* Triptych. 1805–6.

the rush for shelter, and makes a pass at a young fop, who seems nothing displeased to have been thrown into such pleasant company by the passing storm. And to the right, two girls under a single umbrella, and their poorly-clad attendant, dash helter-skelter for the cover of the tree.

In the one entitled *The Fishing Net*, Utamaro makes wonderful use of his favourite 'veiling' device. This is another night-piece, with a waning moon high in the dark sky (Fig. 108). A pleasure-boat with its crew of beautiful girls and *sake*-drinking male companions has drawn alongside a fishing craft, just as the fisherman heaves his huge net, framed on a cross of bamboo poles, out of the water. The girls simulate a lively interest in the fisherman's catch—no more than a poor single fish for all the immense net—but in contrast to their forced animation, a young man sits undisturbed in the pleasure-boat, and pours out another cup of *sake*. The mesh of the red net stretches from top to bottom of the picture with charming effects of colour-change on the pinks and purples of the dresses of those seen through it, whilst the bold soaring curves of the bamboo frame contrive to draw the scattered groups into a harmonious whole.

To the end of his days, Utamaro records the picnics and the pleasure outings that were a feature of Edo life. One triptych, with the seal date 1804, depicts a cherry-viewing party at Gotenyama, a place near Edo that was a rendezvous at this season of the year. Another, of about the same time or later, *Girls on the beach at Ise*, shows a band of nine girls greeting the dawn in view of the twin needle-like rocks known as 'Husband-and-Wife' and linked together by the fanciful Japanese with plaited straw rope.[1] One girl joins her hands in prayer as the red sun looms up between the two rocks, some are paddling in the surf, others slip off their sandals to follow them.

And in the year of his death, Utamaro was still drawing the beauties of the Green Houses to whom he remained faithful all his working life, and in whose houses he was no doubt by this time *persona grata*. A print with the seal-date of 1806, depicting the reception-room of the House of the Fan, is of particular interest in that, on the right, partially obscured by an attendant carrying a *samisen*, we get a glimpse of the very wall-painting of a Hō-ō bird that Utamaro is shown executing in the last print

[1] These rocks were held in veneration and it was almost a matter of religious observance to be present to view the sun as it rose between them. One is reminded of our own pilgrimages to Stonehenge at dawn.

of the *Annals of the Green Houses*. The young belles sit in a half-circle in their finest robes and with their hair transfixed, in the ugly style of this time, with quivers of broad pins. Before them are little stands for their belongings and around them hover servant girls in the fan-patterned 'livery' of the house, ready to attend to the *oirans'* behests. Interesting as it is, this triptych has practically none of the qualities that come to mind when we think of an Utamaro print. It is a competent enough production, but the divine spark was quite extinguished in the artist who designed it.

I have deferred mentioning to the last the two triptychs that depict the whole trade of print-making and publishing, since although probably a year or two earlier than the print last described, they bring to a close this brief selection of late triptychs fittingly, concerned as they are with the craft that over a period of thirty years had produced literally thousands of prints from the master's drawings and so enriched not only the Edo dwellers of the time, but all those who, in after times, East and West, have come to admire the art of Utamaro.

As has already been told, women alone are shown performing the various occupations, even the artist himself being impersonated by a girl. Both triptychs are entitled *Edo meibutsu nishiki-e kōsaku* ('*Making the colour-prints for which Edo is famous*').

The first shows the interior of the engraver's workshop, in which one girl, with the cutting knife held upright in her hand, is ready to commence cutting round the design pasted on a block; another is cleaning out the wood between the cut lines with a chisel and mallet, and a third sharpening a knife on a stone. To the left a woman is sizing paper with a brush, and others are hanging sheets up to dry. To the right a girl is holding up a print for inspection whilst a companion brings a cup of tea to a third, representing Utamaro, seated at the table. On the table are letters, addressed to the artist, letters from publishers urgently requesting him to furnish them with designs (Fig. 4).

The companion triptych depicts a publisher's print-shop in Edo. If the print is to be believed, the printing of the sheets went on in a room alongside the booth where the prints were exposed for sale, and the fortunate purchasers could witness an Utamaro print coming to life before their eyes. Two girls are engaged in printing, another brings a block

and fresh supplies of paper. A boy is about to unpack a parcel of prints, and all around is hung a wonderful display of prints in both the ordinary and the *hashirakake* sizes, in that mint state a collector may dream about but never see. On the left, one assistant is handling a packet of Utamaro's *Kintoki* prints just like any other parcel of merchandise, and another is rolling up a print for a customer, probably the young man standing in front of the publisher's sign-board advertising 'Picture Books and Music Books'.

The pressing commissions from the publishers, littering the table in the first of these prints, were probably exhibited as a matter of pride, but no doubt represent only too accurately one of the causes of the deterioration in Utamaro's art. En-

108. *The Fishing Net.* Triptych. About 1804.

feebled by constant industry and possibly by dissipation as well, the imprisonment and the ignominy attendant upon it *may* have hastened the decay of a constitution never, perhaps, over-strong: though it is hard to think of Utamaro as a man likely to be seriously affected by a show of displeasure by the authorities. Be that as it may, it was at this very time of his life when, at the height of his popularity and with no serious contender save Toyokuni to his pre-eminence among the print-designers, the publisher most needed his designs. Thus harassed, it is small wonder that invention and skill should begin to fail or that pupils should have been enlisted to complete the details of designs he no longer had the strength or will to carry through to the end. But it is no difficult matter to separate these later 'studio'

works from the main body of his prints; they can be rejected, whether his own or not, and his reputation safely left to the vast body of prints that are unmistakably his own, the work of the true, the *Shōmei*, Utamaro.

When Utamaro died in the latter part of 1806, the Ukiyo-e school of artists had already reached the lowest ebb of its fortunes since its beginnings in the seventeenth century. Most of those whom we might call the 'classical' masters of the late eighteenth century, those whose work was imbued with the spirit of the earlier formulators of its style from Moronobu to Harunobu, and who had been supported by a high degree of craftsmanship among the engraver and printers—Kiyonaga, Shunshō, Shunchō, Shigemasa, Kitao Masanobu—were either

109. *The Seven Eccentrics of Drunkenness.*
Part of a triptych. About 1795.

rapidly degenerated after a beginning that had had so much promise, into a mass-producer of coarsely-drawn and vilely-coloured actor-prints that now seemed to the taste, the much vitiated taste, of the Edo public. Utamaro's pupils were capable only of reproducing the mannerisms of the master's last and least characteristic phase, and their work rarely rose above mediocrity. It was left to Hokusai and later to Hiroshige to restore the school to something of its former glory, and both these artists excelled in landscape which, until their advent, had been only of secondary importance in the work of the Ukiyo-e school.

As to the causes of the decline in the art of the colour-print at this period, we have to look further than to the individual artists, and seek them rather in a change in the people for whom the prints were produced. In the rapidly expanding town of Edo, the population now included a far higher proportion than formerly of people without the taste or the education to appreciate the refinement of subject, the artistry of design and colour, habitual to the earlier prints: lower standards prevailed among the people, and as was natural, the artists stooped to the level of their patrons.

Utamaro, by virtue both of seniority and merit, happened to be the leader of the school at this crisis in its affairs, but it is unreasonable to blame him, as some have, for the decline in the standards of the Ukiyo-e print-designers, to mark him down as the evil influence that led to the fall. He, more than any, stood out against the general trend, and even in his last years produced prints that, whilst not comparable with his own earlier work, yet were often on a high level of accomplishment and certainly outstanding among contemporary prints from other hands.

dead or had retired from active print-designing, turning their energies to other pursuits, Eishi to painting, Masanobu to literature, Kiyonaga—to shopkeeping. Toyokuni, who had had his upbringing in the halcyon days of the nineties,

BIBLIOGRAPHY

In every general book on Japanese prints, and in most exhibition and sale catalogues, there is material relating to Utamaro, and this Bibliography would be inordinately long if all were included. It is therefore confined to books and articles dealing specifically with Utamaro and his work.

Goncourt, E. de, *Outamaro: Le Peintre des Maisons Vertes.* Paris, 1891.

Bing, S., 'Art of Utamaro'. *The Studio*, No. 4. London, 1895.

Kurth, J., *Utamaro.* Leipzig, 1907.

Vignier-Inada Catalogue, Vol. IV: *Utamaro. Estampes Japonaises . . . exposées au Musée des Arts Décoratifs en Janvier 1912. Catalogue dressé par M. Vignier avec la collaboration de M. Inada. Préface de R. Koechlin.* Paris, 1912.

Goyō, Hachiguchi, *Utamaro no e ni tsuite* ('Concerning Utamaro's Designs'). *Bijutsu Shimpō.* Tokyo, 1914–16.

Chōyō, Hoshino, *Utamaro no bosho ayobi kakochō hakken* ('The discovery of Utamaro's grave and family death-register'). *Ukiyo-e*, Nos. 27 and 37. Tokyo, 1917.

Sexton, J. J. O'Brien, 'Illustrated Books of Japan – II: Utamaro's Books on Natural History'. *The Burlington Magazine*, Vol. XXXII, No. CLXXX. London, 1918.

Noguchi, Yone, *Utamaro.* Tokyo and London, about 1925.

Noguchi, Yone, *Utamaro, Hokusai, Hiroshige.* Tokyo, 1926.

Kazuo, Inoue, *Utamaro Ukiyo-e Shū* (The Memorial Exhibition Catalogue, mounted by the Ukiyo-e Society of Japan). Afterword by I. Kazuo. Tokyo, 1926.

Ukiyo-e Taika Shūsei, Vol. 12: *Kitagawa Utamaro.* Tokyo, 1926.

Odaka, Sennosuke, *Utamaro ehon kū* ('A Study of Utamaro's Picture-Books'). *Ukiyoye no Kenkyu*, No. 20. Tokyo, 1928.

Noguchi, Yone, *L'Art au Japon: Utamaro.* Paris, 1928.

Shibui, Kiyoshi, 'Kurth's and de Goncourt's *Utamaro*: The Problems of the Study of his Erotic Works'. *Ukiyoye no Kenkyu*, No. 22. Tokyo, 1928.

Gonkaru no Utamaro ('Goncourt's *Utamaro*'), translated by Yone Noguchi. Tokyo, 1929.

Kazuo, Inoue, *Utamaro* (in *Ukiyo-e Hyōjin Gashū* series). Tokyo, 1930.

Kenji, Toda, *Descriptive Catalogue of Japanese and Chinese Illustrated Books in the Ryerson Library of the Art Institute of Chicago.* Chicago, 1931.

Takimizawa Woodcut Institute, *Rare Colour-Prints by Utamaro.* Tokyo, 1931.

Noguchi, Yone, *Utamaro* (in the series *Rokudai Ukiyo-e Shū Kettei-han*, 'Six Great Ukiyo-e Masters'). Tokyo, 1932.

Kazuo, Inoue, *Utamaro no Dozō Sagami no Oborozuki* ('Utamaro's *Hazy Moon at Dozō, Sagami*'). *Ukiyo-e Geijutsu*, No. 9. Tokyo, 1932.

Utamaro no okubi-e nijū-ichi dai ('Twenty-one *Large Head* Prints of Utamaro'). *Ukiyo-e Geijutsu*, No. 9. Tokyo, 1932.

Shibui, Kiyoshi, *Utamaro. Ukiyo-e Geijutsu*, No. 9. Tokyo, 1932.

Kazuo, Inoue, *Utamaro no hanji-e* ('Utamaro's *rebus* prints'). *Ukiyo-e Geijutsu*, No. 9. Tokyo, 1932.

Narazaki, Muneshige, *Ehon sashie yori mitaru Utamaro* ('Utamaro's Illustrations to Picture-Books'). *Ukiyo-e Geijutsu.* Tokyo, 1935.

Kondō, Ichitarō, *Utamaro.* Tōyō Bijutsu Bunko series, No. 42. Tokyo, 1940.

Yoshida, Teruji, *Utamaro Zenshū* ('The Complete Utamaro'). Tokyo, 1941.

Ledoux, L. V., *Japanese Prints Bunchō to Utamaro in the Collection of Louis V. Ledoux.* New York, 1948.

Trotter, Massey, *Catalogue of the Work of Kitagawa Utamaro in the Collection of the New York Public Library.* New York, 1950.

Baltus, George M., *Outamaro.* Catalogue of an Exhibition at the Palais des Beaux-Arts, Brussels. Introduction by G. M. Baltus. Brussels, 1951.

Shibui, Kiyoshi, *Utamaro.* Tokyo, 1952.

Shibui, Kiyoshi, *Utamaro seitan ni-hyaku nen* ('The Utamaro Bicentenary'). *Nihon Bijutsu Kogei*, No. 166. Tokyo, 1952.

Hillier, J. R., *Utamaro.* Catalogue of an Exhibition at the Gemeente Museum, The Hague. Introduction by J. R. Hillier. The Hague, 1953.

Hillier, J. R., 'Japanese Colour-Prints, III: Utamaro'. *Connoisseur*, Vol. CXXXII, No. 534. London, 1953.

Hihan Utamaro ('The "secret publications" of Utamaro') (a study largely of erotic books). Ed. Utamaro Kenkyū Sha. Tokyo, 1953.

Kitagawa Utamaro. British Museum, Dept. of Oriental Antiquities. (A paper prepared as an introduction to the Bicentenary Exhibition at the British Museum, 1953.)

Adhémar, Jean, *Outamaro: Peintures; estampes. Exposition commémorative du bi-centenaire de la naissance de l'artiste.* Introduction by J. Adhémar. Exhibition held at the Huguette Berès Gallery, Paris, 1954.

Winzinger, F., *Kitagawa Utamaro Kurtisanen.* Baden-Baden, 1955.

Hajek, Lubor, *Utamaro: Portraits in the Japanese Woodcut.* London, n.d. English translation of *Utamaro: Das Porträt im Japanischen Holzschnitt.* Prague, 1957.

Shibui, Kiyoshi, *Utamaro ni tsuite* ('About Utamaro'). *Museum*, No. 95. Tokyo, 1955.

Kondō, Ichitarō, *Kitagawa Utamaro.* English adaptation by Charles S. Terry. Kodansha Library of Japanese Art. Tokyo, 1956.

Utamaro hyaku-go-jū kinen Ukiyo-e meisaku ten ('Exhibition of masterworks to commemorate the 150th anniversary of Utamaro's death'). Asahi Shimbun. Tokyo, 1956.

Shibui, Kiyoshi, *Utamaro sanken. Sogo*, 6th month. Tokyo, 1957.

Shibui, Kiyoshi, *Shinobu ga oka Utamaro. Bujutsu Techo*, No. 4. Tokyo, 1958.

Shibui, Kiyoshi, *Utamaro* (in the series Genshokuhan Bijutsu Library, No. 116). Tokyo, 1959.

Kondō, Ichitarō, *Utamaro no bijin-ga* ('Pictures of Beautiful Women by Utamaro'). Tokyo, 1960.

Hillier, J., *Utamaro: Colour Prints and Paintings*, First Edition. London, 1961.

Shibui, Kiyoshi, *Utamaro* (English translation of the 1959 Tokyo edition, see above). Tokyo, 1962.

Kikuchi, Sadao, 'Utamaro's *Musume Hidokei* series'. *Ukiyo-e Art*, No. 1. Tokyo, 1962.

Shibui, Kiyoshi, *Ukiyo-e Zuten*, Vol. 13: *Utamaro*. Tokyo, 1964.

The Work of Utamaro and his Pupils. An Exhibition held at Shirokiya Nihonbashi, Tokyo, April 3rd to 8th 1964. Ukiyo-e Art, No. 6. Tokyo, 1964.

Suzuki, Jūzō, *Utamaro ehon no bunseki-teki kō satsu* ('An Analytical Study of Utamaro's Illustrated Books'). *Ukiyo-e Art*, No. 7. Tokyo, 1964.

Yoshikazu, Hayashi, *Utamaro no saikon setsu* ('Utamaro's second marriage'). *Ukiyo-e Art*, No. 8. Tokyo, 1964.

Exhibition of Masterworks of Utamaro Bicentenary of Nishiki-e. Japan Ukiyo-e Society. Tokyo, 1964.

Hillier, Jack, *Twelve Wood-Block Prints of Kitagawa Utamaro illustrating the Process of Silk-Culture*. The Collection of Edwin and Irma Grabhorn. San Francisco, 1965.

Mitchell, C. H., *Utamaro* (Exhibition Catalogue). Asahi Shimbun. Introduction by C. H. Mitchell. Tokyo, 1965.

Goncourt, E. de, *Utamaro*. Translated into Japanese by Higashi Oji. *Ukiyo-e*, Nos. 13–17. Tokyo, 1965.

Yoshikazu, Hayashi, *Jigoku gokuraku to Utamaro no hihan* ('Hell, Paradise, and Utamaro's "secret" books'). *Ukiyo-e*, No. 19. Tokyo, 1965.

Narazaki, Muneshige (Ed.), *Ukiyo-e bijinga-yakusha-e*, Vol. 4: *Utamaro* (I). Tokyo, 1965.

Kikuchi, Sadao (Ed.), *Ukiyo-e bijinga-yakusha-e*, Vol. 5: *Utamaro* (II). Tokyo, 1965.

Kikuchi, Sadao, *Utamaro* (I), in the *Nihon Meisaku Zenshū* series. Tokyo, 1966.

Narazaki, Muneshige, *Utamaro* (II), in the *Nihon Meisaku Zenshū* series. Tokyo, 1967.

Narazaki, Muneshige, and Kikuchi, Sadao, *Masterworks of Ukiyo-e: Utamaro*. English translation by John Bester. Tokyo, 1968.

Shibui, Kiyoshi, *Utamaro no sekkai* ('The World of Utamaro'). Tokyo, 1968.

Sekkai no Utamaro Ten ('World Exhibition of the Works of Utamaro'). Exhibition Catalogue. Tokyo, 1970.

Ukiyo-e, No. 45. Special Utamaro Issue. Tokyo, 1971.

Shibui, Kiyoshi, and Kikuchi, Sadao, *Utamaro* (in *Zenshū Ukiyo-e Hanga* series). Tokyo, 1971.

Utamaro Kikō-hyakusen ten ('Exhibition of 100 Rare Works of Utamaro'). Ukiyo-e Hozon. Tokyo, 1971.

Ukiyo-e Taikei, Vol. 5: *Utamaro*. Tokyo, 1971.

Narazaki, Muneshige (Ed.), *Zaigai Hihō* (Treasures in Foreign Collections), Vol. 5: *Kitagawa Utamaro*. Tokyo, 1972.

Keyes, Roger T., *Kitagawa Utamaro sakuhin mokuroku* ('Catalogue of Works by Kitagawa Utamaro'). In *Zaigai Hihō*, Vol. 5: *Kitagawa Utamaro*. Tokyo, 1972.

Ukiyo-e Taikei, Vol. 5: *Utamaro*. Tokyo, 1973.

Utamaro and Hiroshige from the Honolulu Academy of Arts, James A. Michener Collection. Exhibition Catalogue. Tokyo, 1976.

Baba, Ichiro, and Shibui, Kiyoshi, *Utamaro*. The Sun Special Issue De Luxe Edition. Tokyo, 1977.

Utamaro no Meisaku Soroemono ('Utamaro's Famous Series'). *Ukiyo-e*, No. 70. Tokyo, 1977.

A sake party. Brush drawing for a fan
by Utamaro (left), Shikimaro (centre) and Utagawa Kuninao (right).
About 1804–6. Haifa, Israel, Tikotin Museum of Japanese Art.